Through the heartbreak testimony reveals a tender and compassionate God who has not altered His covenant with him and his two children. Has your vision been shattered by some unexpected circumstance? This story will fill you with courage and renewed hope at God's ability to bring beauty out of ashes.

—John Dawson
President, Youth With A Mission
Author of *Healing America's Wounds*

There is nothing more debilitating than a wounded or broken heart, yet God is the one who mends our hearts and shows us His greater purposes for the moments of pain and challenge. In *Unwilling to Concede*, Brad Stanley has wonderfully captured both the promise and plight of our emerging generation that I, too, wrote about in 1994 in *The Fatherless Generation*. Bringing hope to a generation living in a world where dreams die daily, Brad's message was birthed through the crucibles of experience and the tragic loss of his own dreams when his wife Sherry went to be with Jesus in the prime of her life and in the midst of their thriving ministry.

As Brad and his family have learned, there is life beyond the heartache and pain of loss as we recognize the greater legacy and destiny of our journeys. I encourage you to read this book with a sense of God's greater purpose for your own journey and to remember that no challenge is too difficult for the Lord as we keep our vision of hope on a God who keeps His promises!

—Dr. J. Doug Stringer
President, Turning Point Ministries Intl./
Somebody Cares America
Author of *Who's Your Daddy Now?*

Brad Stanley is not only a wild-eyed visionary with a passion to reach the remaining unreached people groups in our generation, he is a practical missionary who has been living his life embracing the ethnic peoples of Chicago. *Unwilling to Concede* is full of the revelation of our Redeemer God who loves to restore broken lives and broken dreams in the broken cities of America.

—Dick Bashta
Mission Pastor, Living Stones Church,
Crown Point, Indiana
Director, GlobalROAR

UNWILLING TO CONCEDE

BRAD STANLEY

CREATION
HOUSE

A STRANG COMPANY

UNWILLING TO CONCEDE by Brad Stanley
Published by Creation House
A Strang Company
600 Rinehart Road
Lake Mary, Florida 32746
www.creationhouse.com

Unless otherwise noted, all Scripture quotations are from the Holy Bible, New International Version. Copyright © 1973, 1978, 1984, International Bible Society. Used by permission.

Scripture quotations marked KJV are from the King James Version of the Bible.

Scripture quotations marked NAS are from the New American Standard Bible—Updated Edition, Copyright © 1960, 1962, 1963, 1968, 1971, 1972, 1973, 1975, 1977, 1995 by The Lockman Foundation. Used by permission. (www.Lockman.org)

Scripture quotations marked NKJV are from the New King James Version of the Bible. Copyright © 1979, 1980, 1982 by Thomas Nelson, Inc., publishers. Used by permission.

Greek and Hebrew definitions are derived from *Strong's Exhaustive Concordance of the Bible, with Hebrew, Chaldee, and Greek Dictionaries*, Nashville, TN: Thomas Nelson Publishers, 1984.

Design Director: Bill Johnson
Cover designer: Karen Grindley

Library of Congress Control Number: 2008923828
International Standard Book Number: 978-1-59979-369-6

First Edition

08 09 10 11 12 — 9 8 7 6 5 4 3 2 1
Printed in the United States of America

In memory of Sherry Stanley,
born into this world on December 10, 1964,
taken to her true home on December 25, 2003.

Honoring God in life,
He has honored her in His presence.

Dedicated to our kids,
Jordan and Joseph Stanley,
who have chosen to love God
in spite of their loss.

ACKNOWLEDGMENTS

WRITING THIS BOOK was both difficult and inspiring—difficult because of the personal reflection needed to articulate the brokenness that had entered my world, but overwhelmingly encouraging because of the generosity of the Lord to give me His perspective. I am most grateful to the Lord for being a God who communicates and for truly showing me how committed He is to us. Thank You, Lord, for giving my family such an amazing reason to continue living.

There have been many people who have invested in my life over the years, making it possible for my family to navigate through our loss and see the nature and character of God. I am very grateful for the Youth With A Mission family that have invested so much in my life, especially the YWAM leaders and staff of Tyler, Texas. Thank you, Leland and Fran Paris, for giving so much love, trust, and support to my family. Thanks to Mary Brock for her early content suggestions and Gillian Rourke for her editing help with the first manuscript. Most importantly, thank you to Ron and Evelyn Moyer for all the support in getting this book published. Thanks, Ron, for letting me unload on you all the thoughts in this book while stuck in China on the way to Mongolia. Without your insistence that I write this book, it may not have happened.

Thanks to the YWAM staff at our own ministry in Chicago, who have provided a wonderful community for my kids and a great support for God's call on our lives. Thanks for laying down your lives for the Lord. You have encouraged my family greatly. Finally, thank you to the many people I encountered over the last few years who grasped God's unwillingness to concede His purpose in their lives and are still living His story, in spite of their loss and brokenness. You are my heroes. May this become the pervasive characteristic of this generation.

CONTENTS

INTRODUCTION

OVER THE LAST twenty years serving full-time in Youth With A Mission, I have had the privilege to work alongside an army of very dedicated Christians from many different backgrounds and churches. I have seen a generation of passionate believers emerge. As with every generation, there are unique giftings and characteristics that can be seen. I believe this generation has wonderful gifts of faith, worship, and relevant evangelism. These are the very tools needed to face what some have called "the last of the giants" in world missions.

Though I believe these are the characteristics the Lord sees, the world has defined this generation in other terms. They are the children of broken homes and broken commitments—the first generation in history to have more marriages end in divorce than remain together. With modern media channels, the average person is also acutely aware of gross suffering around the world. We are overwhelmed, not only by losses in our own lives but by countless devastations and evils in the lives of those around us. The pain that many feel is more than they can handle. More people die from suicide each year than from homicide, and suicide is now the third leading cause of death among young adults in America. A study by the Substance Abuse and Mental Health Services Administration reported that close to three million adolescents age twelve to seventeen "considered" suicide in 2000, and one-third of those attempted to end their lives.[1]

Several years ago, while living in an inner-city tenant building, my wife and I heard a serious domestic fight break out in one of the apartments down the hall. As we quickly went to see what was going on, we were confronted by an image that I will never be able to forget. The door to the apartment was open, and as a man and woman verbally and physically slapped each other around, there in the hall stood two small children aged four and seven. They stood very still with their heads down. They were frozen, waiting for the pain to stop.

Perhaps you can identify with those two kids. Pain and loss have a way of immobilizing us on the inside. Regardless of what our heart and mind tell us to do, we just shut down. The enemy you face may not be a lack of heart but a lack of confidence. Loss can be a thief that robs our most treasured possessions: the ability to take risks, to be vulnerable, and to commit to something. The gifts of God to this generation are threatened by the loss of these things. Without the ability to take risks, faith will be fruitless. Without vulnerability, there is no true worship. We must be a generation of long and committed obedience if we are to carry the heart of God in a relevant way to the nations.

I became personally aware of this when my wife and partner, Sherry, died at age thirty-nine on Christmas Day, 2003, after battling cancer for only four months. It's like getting the breath knocked out of you. As a twelve year old in junior high school, I remember standing in a ring of kids preparing to fight a bully that had been taunting me for several days. He gave the first punch, perfectly placed in the center of my stomach. As I looked him in the face, my heart and mind wanted to hit back and leave a mark that he would not forget, but I could not move. I was immobilized. It was the same feeling I felt as I stood in the middle of the street outside the back doors of the ambulance that held the body of my best friend. Something had gone terribly wrong. It wasn't supposed to be this way. It wasn't in the plans. Sherry and I had enjoyed a great and intimate relationship, one with purpose and dreams of serving the Lord as a family in missions. She dreamt my dreams with me, increased my faith, and brought a God-intended joy to my life.

Every God-given gift to us becomes an intimate partner in fulfilling His destiny in our lives, whether it's relationships that God brings into our lives or the things that He has given each of us, such as innocence, wholeness, and destiny. When these things are lost, the dreams and visions for your life go through a long, agonizing death. Every day after Sherry died was another realization of all that had been taken from me. You can never grasp all that has been lost in the moment it is taken away. Time can become an enemy. It becomes a constant reminder of what's not there and how broken you feel. These reminders mock your ability to go on. My life was broken, and I couldn't move. How was I to keep going? How was I to help my nine-year-old daughter, Jordan, and my six-year-old son, Joseph, write their stories with God without their mother?

This is not a book I ever intended to write. Over the last four years since Sherry went to be with Jesus, I have questioned and contemplated many things with the Lord. What has come out of that is this book. This is written as an encouragement for those who are living with a separation from their God-intended story, and hopefully as a guide for those who will experience it in the future. These separations can produce an intense amount of grief. Yet, this is not a book to manage grief. There are many books on that subject, some of which have been my good friends over the last few years. The profound effect that grief has on the individual is something that poets, writers, and theologians will never be able to capture fully. It is perhaps one of the greatest arguments for the eternality of the human soul. The gravity of grief exists because our souls tell us that we were made to walk with eternity; that our very make-up was never meant to be separated from certain things. Yet, every person that has set out on this journey of life has and will experience loss and the separation from those things that God never intended us to be separated from. For many, that separation takes place through the tragic death of loved ones. For others it is the tragic separation from wholeness, innocence, or the hope of a life of purpose and meaning. This generation is threatened by the immobilizing effect of mounting loss.

This is also not a book that says, "You should just get over it!" The irony of grief and loss is that they cry out for someone to understand, identify, and comfort, yet its effect is so intimate that it can never truly be shared with any other person. I do not believe that grief or pain is something that we grow out of as much as it is something that we learn to integrate into our lives. God will travel with us in our loss. Yet God is not only compassionate but also redemptive by nature. Often, we are unaware of the authority we have to release. It is found in His redemptive nature in our circumstances. This is a book written to a generation of great promise threatened by great loss, one that desires to know the redemptive power of our God.

As I sought the Lord in how to respond to my loss, I was overwhelmed by the emphasis of Scripture in revealing God as a redeemer. The Bible reveals a God who responds to our losses with a strong commitment to redeem, restore, and finish what He has destined for our lives. This strong aspect of God's character and the way in which He relates to our fallen and broken world affects the way we will respond and relate to our brokenness and the brokenness of those around us. We are invited in Scripture to celebrate God's redeeming nature and embrace the honor of becoming co-redeemers with Him. My hope is that those of you who have had the breath knocked out of you will find strength to finish writing your story with the Lord.

PART I

DISCOVERING
OUR REDEEMER

I know that my Redeemer lives.

—JOB 19:25—

CHAPTER 1

HOPE

*I pray also that the eyes of your heart may be enlightened
in order that you may know the hope to which he has called
you, the riches of his glorious inheritance in the saints,
and his incomparably great power for us who believe.*

—EPHESIANS 1:18–19—

*Hope deferred makes the heart sick, but a
longing [dream] fulfilled is a tree of life.*

—PROVERBS 13:12—

MOST OF US have distinct memories of our past when we felt like time stood still; those moments when something is seen, felt, heard, or experienced that makes a lasting impact on the rest of our lives. There is one memory in my mind that has always left such a clear impression that I feel at times as if it were yesterday. I was eight years old, riding in the car with my family. I don't remember where we were going or where we came from, but I remember such a feeling of satisfaction. My mom and dad were in the front seat. I was in the back with my older brother and sister. Everything felt right in my world. I felt such happiness that I remember not being able to contain myself. In my eight-year-old way I spoke up in the car and declared that God had really blessed us because we had the perfect family. The car got quiet for a moment after a few smiles from Mom and Dad, and then everything resumed as usual. It was the first time that I can remember feeling that life was truly good. I felt at that moment as if I could accomplish anything. My dreams got bigger, and I somehow believed that life was worth living

Three years later my dad died in a tragic car accident, followed by years of difficult transition and loss in my family. Loss has a way of stealing, or at least hiding in a cruel way, those moments when we truly believed that life had a purpose and was worth living. Where does that hope and confidence come from? Why should we expect that something of value and worth should come from our lives? Why do we dream, as children, about futures full of promise and glory when we have so many examples of pain and suffering around us?

One of the privileges of being in missions is the opportunity to witness people from so many diverse cultures and lifestyles. Over the years, I have seen people living in some of the worst conditions, conditions of extreme poverty or sickness. Often I have wondered how some could survive such an existence. It's the children that always made the most impact on me. Interestingly, the youngest of children seemed to have the ability to experience some happiness in their world. Many were living in slums, on the streets, or in hospitals. Yet often I felt as though I could see that same thought of hope, expectation, and dreaming in the eyes of these children that I had as an eight year old in the back of the family car. Regardless of the circumstances we are born into, we all dream as children of great accomplishments, happy families, and the chance to make a mark on our world. As the years go by though, those dreams are often shattered. They are challenged by all the loss we experience, as well as the reality of devastating loss in the world around us. It is possible that one of the most threatening results of loss is the death of hope and expectation on our lives.

THE ABILITY TO DREAM

Is it just the cruel reality of naïveté that allows kids to dream and hope when what lies around the corner for their lives is extreme hardship and difficulty? I have come to believe that it is actually a part of our nature to somehow expect that our lives could experience great accomplishment and glory. There is something within all of us that believes we are not only meant for glory but that it is somehow possible. From the moment we learn to imagine, we are dreaming of great adventures, daring feats, and heroic accomplishments. Perhaps this capacity to dream and expect great purpose for our lives is a gift from God. It reinforces the reality that we were made for intimacy with God and His dreams. It's a road map that is meant to give us the fuel we need to discover God's unique and valuable purpose for our lives. Without it we not only lose our drive to live but can be forced to live without truly living.

The loss of my father as a child challenged my God-given ability to expect, dream, and anticipate the future. The tragic loss of loved ones, stolen innocence, and shattered lives threaten our capacity to hope in the goodness of God for our future. The apostle Paul spoke of the need for the eyes of our heart to be enlightened. Through sin and the effects of this fallen world in which we live, we have lost the ability to see the amazing call of God on our lives. Paul called it God's glorious inheritance for those who believe. (See Ephesians 1:18.) To live life under the constant hope and anticipation of great things with God is a part of our design. God intended our lives to exist with the persistent companion of expectation, the expectation that God is unfolding great significance and purpose for our lives, the anticipation that every new day brings the promise of increasing intimacy with God, and the glory of being caretakers and benefactors of all that is eternally valuable.

This expectation is so much a part of our created makeup that it is self-destructive to exist without it. When we lose this supreme hope, we can be either forced to live in the constant shadow of depression and despair or driven to create alternative forms of anticipation. The anticipation of this evening's relational rendezvous, this weekend's big event, or even the daily shot at the lottery provide shallow or temporary expectation to life. Still, these things provide the fuel many need to get through another day. The things that we hope for give us reason to exist. Yet because the returns on many of our earthly hopes fall short of defining adequately the glory we know we were created for, we must either live in constant revision of our hopes and dreams or succumb to forms of depression and despair. Depression can be the inability to anticipate any good around the corner. Often those who struggle with depression are just the honest ones. Their perceptive and realistic view on life restricts them from putting any trust in the fleeting alternatives in which many of us place our significance and hope.

Have the cruel reality of loss and the brokenness of your world stolen this hope and confidence in your life? For some of us, that hope was stolen so early that we never set out to discover God's unique call on our lives. We lost our ability to dream or expect something great from our future. As a result, we spend our daily time and effort seeking to experience as much personal happiness as we can until our short life is over. For these individuals, the topic of calling and destiny seems foreign and somewhat elusive. Others of us set out to discover God's personal call on our lives, still believing that we have the ability to do great things for God, only to experience such devastating hurdles along the way that we are either left powerless to finish what we started or left wondering whether we ever should have dreamt such dreams to begin with. For these, the topic of God's call on our lives seems unattainable or perhaps even naïve.

REDISCOVERING OUR GREATNESS

As I have mentioned before, I believe this generation has experienced incredible loss through broken homes, lost loved ones, and gross suffering. Yet there resides within the youth of our day an awareness that they exist to make an impact in the world. How can we rediscover that greatness and see it come to pass when we are threatened by not only the losses of our past but also the looming possibility of increasing global tragedy? Can we truly regain that part of our original design, to live the kind of lives that can be sung in God's presence for all of eternity?

I began to dream again several years after my father died. As a seventeen-year-old, I stood in a crowd of young people watching a Christian concert and listening to the challenge to give my life to God and let Him release His destiny for my life. It was a call to give my life to missions. I was challenged by stories of smuggling Bibles across the iron curtain of communism. They spoke of the need for a generation of young people that could go into the hardest regions of the world and bring the gospel to countless peoples who had never heard it. It was a dream—a dream I had never dreamt for my life and yet a dream that felt so familiar, a dream that seemed to be my own dream but one I had stopped dreaming. That day I heard God's call on my life. I was given back my ability to dream His dreams.

Many of us struggle to hear God's call on our lives. We discover God's call by recognizing first that we were created not merely for the pursuit of personal happiness but to live the adventurous experience of a love relationship with God. This revelation should cause us to slow down long enough to listen to His dreams for the world and rediscover our desire to be a part of those dreams. What happens next is that God begins to paint you into those dreams and you become a dreamer too. The call of God on each of our lives is discovered through this process of intimacy with the Lord and His heart for us and the world. We all have a unique call of God on our lives because we were all made with the purpose of knowing God intimately and sharing in His eternal purposes.

One of God's redemptive goals is to restore our hope in His unique and intimate call on our lives. It's a calling to inherit great purpose and eternal significance. God is a redeemer by nature. When Adam and Eve sinned, God did not decide to just start over but immediately instituted and communicated His plan to redeem and restore His original design for our lives. The life, death, and resurrection of Jesus were the culmination of that plan. One of the things that Jesus died for is our ability to hope again. It is this ability that causes us to set goals of greatness with God in our lives. It is the hope of our calling that restores a daily anticipation toward the fulfillment of those goals, giving definition and motivation for our existence.

Two years after that missions concert I joined Youth With A Mission with about $50 in my pocket and an uncanny expectation that God would actually do in me what He had called me to do. My first overseas missions trip was traveling across China in 1987. We had brought bags full of Bibles and Christian literature into the heart of China. I'll never forget the joy that etched across the face of one underground church leader as we gave him dozens of Bibles. He kept saying over and over, "Thank you, Jesus; thank you, Jesus." Somehow the difficulties of the last several years without my father had no effect on that moment. Nothing could steal what God had let me be a part of. Perhaps the thief was gone. Every day brought more anticipation of what might unfold next.

It was on this outreach that I fell in love with the woman who was to become my wife nearly four years later. Sherry and I spent those next four years working on the same ministry team. We led missionary teams into Mexico, the Caribbean, and South Africa. It was while our ministry team was in Brazil that I asked her if she would be my wife.

Sherry also had discovered the call of God on her life. When I had asked her a year earlier how she would respond if I told her that I was attracted to her, she said with great surety, "I don't know. I need to evaluate whether you would be a distraction from God's plan for my life!" Fortunately, when I asked her to marry me, she had resolved that question with the Lord. When I look back on the day we got married, I remember having that same feeling I had when I was eight years old. Everything seemed right with my world. I felt as though we could accomplish anything. I knew that no matter what the Lord asked of us, we could do it. We dreamt with God, and He was dreaming with us. That hope and expectation seemed impenetrable.

Two weeks after we got married, we were leading a team of twenty-five missionary students across Eastern Europe. Time stood still again one evening while in Romania. We just finished a revival meeting in a small church made of rough concrete blocks and a tin roof. It was freezing outside, but all the doors and windows were open because the church was packed with people and there was a crowd outside as well. It was only months after the fall of Romania's harshest dictator, who had kept Christianity oppressed for years. Half the village seemed to be crammed into this building. At the end of the meeting we brought out about three hundred Bibles in the Romanian language. The people lined up to receive a Bible for the first time. They kept thanking and hugging our team as they held their own Bible in their rough hands. I remember looking down from the platform at my wife. She had that smile that she always got when she was doing the things she loved the most. I have seen that smile in my kids many times, the kind of smile that is unfettered and stretches from ear to ear. She looked at me with a look in her eyes that said, "Can we stay here forever?" At that moment I knew we could do anything that God might ask of us. We had very little money as a married couple, no possessions, and not even our own home, yet we were dreaming with God and He was dreaming with us. Surely nothing could steal that from us.

The following year we were leading a team of eleven to pioneer a long-term YWAM ministry center in Chicago. Those years of pioneering were hard. But we never stopped dreaming with God. That was one of the things that Sherry did well. Her vision kept my vision alive. But so did her laughter, the look on her face when she lay in the warm sun, her ability to analyze anything with great precision, and the goofy games she liked to play. She created fun! Though she did not know it, I would watch her, late at night when the lights were out, dancing for hours in worship just for her lover God. I knew at those times that God was near.

Sherry and I had all the difficulties that married life can bring, such as vulnerability, misunderstanding, and fear. Yet we had the deepest friendship. I had never experienced what love was until I met Sherry. When we were without money or ministry was hard, God kept us dreaming with Him. One of those dreams was to see believers from many different nations trained and released with their unique giftings into world missions. In 2001, Sherry and I led a team of Asian Indians on a short-term missions trip to El Salvador. This was our first all-ethnic team to take to the mission field. Every day on that outreach brought such an overwhelming sense of satisfaction. I knew that this adventure with God was what I was made for. Life for Sherry and me was full of hope and anticipation in the fulfillment of God's call on our lives.

That anticipation continued to grow over the next four years. We dreamt more with God and continued to experience the fulfillment of His calling of intimacy and ministry. Then in the fall of 2003 everything began to change. Sherry was diagnosed with cancer, and in four short months, we had lost her. In a moment, all the hope and anticipation for God's destiny on my family seemed completely threatened.

Perhaps the very reason we experience such great shock in tragedy is because we live life with the anticipation that good is around the corner. What do we do when that hope is disappointed? How do we stave off the sickness our hearts feel when hope is destroyed? We feel mocked, cheated, and even foolish, like a child who, after laughing with his friends, finds out that the joke was on him.

FINDING HOPE AGAIN

It is the heart that becomes sick through great loss and devastation. It's the core of our beliefs, values, and motivation for life that experiences trauma. Trauma describes the effect that extreme shock has on our physical bodies. If you have ever seen someone in physical trauma, you have witnessed a complete shut-down of a person's normal faculties, from his neurological system to his cognitive abilities. When trauma hits, there is no longer any ability to function.

Hope and anticipation in God is similar to our nervous system. It provides the pulse for all effective movement. Without it, we are either living with some form of emotional and spiritual paralysis or experiencing the complete shut-down of a comatose existence. An honest look reveals that much of our world is living in this kind of reality. Ephesians 1:18 declares that it is the eyes of our heart that God wants to give hope back to.

How does God give back to our heart the anticipation that what we were created for can still be accomplished? When we pick up the shattered pieces of ravaged emotions, broken relationships, and the loss of our greatest treasures, how do we regain the hope of God's eternal significance on our earthly lives?

My kids and I have struggled over the last few years since Sherry's death to regain a hope and expectation for our lives. Sherry was in all those hopes and dreams, just like my father was a valuable part of that eight year old's perfect picture of life. It's not the loss of comfort or pleasure that wreaks the most damage. The realization that the world does not revolve around us and that our greatest treasures in life are not found in our personal happiness, does not rob us but rather releases us into maturity. What threatens us most at the core of our being is the fear that our life may not in the end be able to count for eternity. It's the fear that the happiness of God may not be attainable through the broken pieces of our lives that haunt us. It is this threat, this mockery to our existence produced by the shattering effects of loss that shouts in our heads and steals our hope of purpose and fruitfulness for God and His kingdom. How does hope endure through our losses, especially through the loss of those things that were God-intended for our lives? Where, then, is God in the chaos of our broken world? What reasons do we have to continue dreaming and hoping for our lives?

I was sleepless the night of Sherry's death, partly in disbelief at what had just happened, overwhelmed at how I was going to explain this to my kids, and immobilized by the thought of hopelessness. Throughout the following days and months, I continually heard God say to my heart over and over, "I am a Redeemer." Slowly hope returned—hope fueled by the revelation that God was not forced to find a way to start over in my life, but that He was committed and able to continue the story of intimacy and greatness that He had intended for my family to share with Him.

I invite you to go on that journey of discovery throughout the pages of this book. God not only wants to heal the brokenness of this generation but give them the tools by which they can finish writing the stories of His greatness through their lives. We must regain our hope and sense of calling. The eyes of our hearts need to see the inheritance that God has for us, which is able to endure the chaos of brokenness and loss. We cannot afford to live in the shadow of depression, and we must not allow ourselves to survive life by simply living under the anticipation of one shallow pursuit of happiness after another. We can say as Job said in the wake of devastating loss, "I know that my Redeemer lives" (19:25).

Lord, I know that I was created to display Your splendor and beauty, only the eyes of my heart struggle to see it. My heart is sick with shattered hopes. I want to dream again. Father, show me the call that you have for my life. Give me back the confidence of its fulfillment. Set my eyes on You, Jesus, the author and finisher of my faith. I need an understanding of You in my loss. Please, Lord, give me eyes to see through this cloud of pain.

CHAPTER 2

A PARTNER IN SORROW

When Jesus saw her weeping, and the Jews who had
come along with her also weeping, he was deeply moved
in spirit and troubled. "Where have you laid him?" he
asked. "Come and see, Lord," they replied. Jesus wept.

—JOHN 11:33–35—

T HOUGH ALL SUFFERING is unique in its effect on the individual, pain and suffering have a way of isolating you. When the doctor came out of the intensive care unit to inform me that they had done all they could for Sherry but could not bring her back, I was then invited to go alone to her bedside. The doctor said to take all the time I needed. I will never forget the feeling of aloneness as I sat by her bed staring at the empty shell of the woman who had known me better than anyone and shared all my dreams. I stared around the room at the medical instruments no longer making any sound. There was a deafening silence. I felt utterly alone. There is a sense in which we know that we are not alone because we know that God is always there. But even if there is someone near us, if we are the only one grieving, we are still alone in our grief.

If we are to look at God's commitment to bring redemption out of our loss and the brokenness of the world around us, we must start with a look at how God feels about our suffering. There have been many books written about this subject, and I do not intend to look at it exhaustively here. What's important is that we recognize what perhaps cannot be known while seeking to represent rightly what can. I would like to suggest that God has not left us alone in our grief but is actually a partner in our sorrow.

Perhaps you have experienced aloneness at difficult times of pain and tragedy. For some it is every night before they go to bed, recounting the broken relationships, the lost loved ones, abusive parent, or nightmarish tragedy that was endured. For others it's just a numbness that seems to accompany them into every part of their lives. As time goes by it becomes a secret but loud reality that is tucked away in some small corner of our existence. The world expects us to just get over it. Worse yet, we somehow feel that God expects the same. This only compounds our feeling of being alone. I knew enough about the Lord to know that He was near me. But somehow I experienced an aloneness in His presence that was never there before. People surrounded me all the time, yet none of them could enter my world. No matter how much they themselves had experienced some loss, they could not identify with mine. I felt utterly alone.

When I would turn to the Lord in my thoughts, I longed to share my grief with Him. I didn't need someone to just *listen* to my grief but to *share* it. During those first sleepless nights I began to sense that the Lord was grieving with me.

When you relive the painful experiences of your past, where is God during those times? Do you perceive Him as aware but indifferent? Is He an observer in your grief? Do you perceive Him as somewhat sensitive to what you are going through but impatient with how long it is taking you to "get over it"? This isolation in our grief not only hinders our intimacy with God but also impacts the effectiveness of our service to Him. Our grief and loss is something that God desires to integrate into our relationship with Him. A generation unable to see God accurately in their grief will be a generation robbed of its ability to display God accurately to a hurting world.

JESUS WEPT

The story recounted to us in John 11:17–44 is a profound glimpse into God's reaction toward our broken world. In situations like this we must remind ourselves that we are not merely looking at Jesus' humanity, but we are looking at the Father Himself. In John 14:8–9, Philip, with what seems to be mounting frustration, says to Jesus, "Lord, show us the Father and that will be enough for us." Jesus answered, "Don't you know me Philip, even after I have been among you such a long time? Anyone who has seen me has seen the Father. How can you say, 'show us the Father'?" In the story of Lazarus we must remember that it was not only Jesus who wept, but the Father as well. The Creator of the universe wept. The All-powerful felt pain. Something was terribly wrong!

John 11:33 says that Jesus was "deeply moved in spirit and troubled." The Greek word here is *embrimaomal*, which means "to have indignation on; to groan with anger." There is actually a connotation that suggests the feeling of injustice. Jesus was disturbed by what He saw. Jesus knew that Lazarus was soon to be raised to life again. His reaction was not from a sense of powerlessness but that of brokenness over what He saw in those around him. It was simply not supposed to be this way. This was not what God intended for His creation. Something had been disrupted; the universe had fallen from its intended glory. Death, loss, and suffering had never been His plan for you and me. Have you ever been "deeply moved in spirit and troubled" over circumstances in your life or the lives of those around you? You are not alone!

The brokenness of God's heart over the state of His creation is so profound. Since Sherry's death, I have learned to share my pain with

God. It is not a sharing by which I simply confess what I am going through but a true sharing in which we weep together. Interestingly, when I weep with the Lord over my loss, I always seem to walk away with a sense that He has lost more and is experiencing a pain over my broken world that far surpasses mine. Have you wept with God lately—not a self-consumed pity party but an intimate time of sharing in the pain you both feel over your fallen, broken world? When we grieve alone, it tends to end in feelings of helplessness, despair, and depression. When God grieves over His creation, it always leads to action. Don't be surprised if after you have wept with God and the tears begin to dry, you hear Him gently say, "Now, let's do something about it!"

Over the last several years I have talked with hundreds of people on the streets of my city. A common question has been, Where was God when I suffered? If we do not portray the suffering heart of God over our fallen world, then we not only lessen His glory, but we steal the very heart out of His redemptive message for mankind. The struggle between the existence of pain and suffering and the existence of a loving God has become the struggle of this generation. It could be argued that there has been more destruction of human life in this generation than any time in history. We are living in the emergence of what is now being called the media generation. The access of global visual and real-time information has made the average person over-whelmingly aware of constant suffering around the world. How do we articulate the nature and character of God to a hurting world as well as address the suffering we ourselves feel?

There are usually three questions asked when experiencing tragic loss and suffering: Why did this happen? How does the Lord feel about it? and What do we do now? Often, if we misrepresent the first and second questions, we will be unable to see God's desire to be involved in the third. It would seem that because of the complexity of free-will creatures, along with the frustrated and decaying world in which we live, we simply do not have the capacity to understand all the dynamics that would answer the first. But the Bible is quite clear on answering the other two, although there have been different ways of interpreting God's involvement in the suffering that we experience. What Scripture allows us to fully know is that God is both frustrated and hurt by the suffering we experience, so much so that He jealously desires to do something about it. Yet, we will be unable to see that jealous commitment if we hold to wrong ideas of how God approaches suffering in general. I would like to suggest a few misconceptions that can hinder us from recognizing God's amazing response to our broken world.

Isn't It All a Part of His Plan?

Shortly after Sherry's death I was told by well-intentioned individuals, "I guess it's all in His master plan," or "We'll just have to find God's hidden meaning," or "His ways are higher than our ways." Much of this line of thinking comes from Isaiah 55:8–9.

> "For my thoughts are not your thoughts, neither are your ways my ways," declares the LORD. "As the heavens are higher than the earth, so are my ways higher than your ways and my thoughts than your thoughts."

I would like to suggest that the use of this scripture to help us accept everything that we do not understand as being from the Lord is a misunderstanding of the context in which it was given. After all, it was not spoken to address the mystery of a difficult situation but to show that God's ways are different than the evil intents of a wicked man's heart. Verse 7 reads,

Let the wicked forsake his way and the evil man his thoughts.
Let him turn to the LORD, and he will have mercy on him, and
to our God, for he will freely pardon.

This was a message to sinners that God is not only different than
us but His ways are even merciful. The conclusion of this passage in
Isaiah is that God is not like the evil, unrelenting tyrants of the world.
Rather, His ways are as separate to those of evil men as the heavens
are higher than the earth. God's character is never shrouded in Scripture and, as Jeremiah 29:13 tells us, we are not only encouraged to
seek His face but promised to find Him if we seek Him with all our
heart. Exodus 33:13 says, "Teach me your ways so I may…find favor
with you." David said in Psalm 51:10–13, "Create in me a pure heart O
God…then I will teach transgressors your ways, and sinners will turn
back to you." We are not only to be familiar with the ways of the Lord,
but they should be tools by which we win sinners back to the amazing
God that we know.

Recently, I came across a statement made by a theologian named
William Sloane Coffin Jr. After the tragic loss of his son Alexander in
a car accident, he came to some conclusions about the Lord's involvement that I believe articulates well what can and cannot be known
during times of loss. He said:

> The one thing that should never be said when someone dies is,
> "It is God's will." Never do we know enough to say that. My
> own condition lies in knowing that it was not the will of God
> that [let] Alex die; that when the waves closed over the sinking
> car, God's heart was the first of all our hearts to break.[1]

The book of Job is another example in which we feel that we are challenged to not question God. We will talk more about this fascinating
book in another chapter, but I find it interesting that when God finally
answers Job's questioning of His justice, God does not say to Job that

he just simply cannot understand what God is like but that he cannot understand the complexity of the universe that God is governing. I do not believe that it is God's character that is a mystery but the way in which He balances the management of chaos in our fallen world with our intended purpose as those created in the image of God. In other words, God is now forced to manage the consequences of our fallen and broken world, brought about through the will of His creation, without violating or destroying His intended purpose for those made in His image and endowed with a unique calling to walk in a loving and colaboring relationship with Him. God remains committed to redeeming man's original intent, while in His mercy He places a limit on man's suffering by limiting the duration of our fallen world's existence. It is not His character that we are unable to understand but the amazing way in which God is maintaining His original intent for mankind in spite of our fallen and broken world. Job simply could not have had the reference point that God had of the universe and therefore the capacity to understand all the complex variables that led up to his situation.

Amazingly, the Scripture tells us that Job did not sin or curse God through such great suffering, declaring that famous verse, "I know that my Redeemer lives" (Job 19:25). Yet as time went on he struggled with God's justice, seeing Him as the sole orchestrator of his circumstances. In the end, Job repents of these accusations as he comes face to face with God. Perhaps Job's greatest misjudgment was in assuming that the only players in this story were he and God. It seems that it was this simplistic view that God was so quick to address. Jesus' instruction for us to pray that God's will would be done on the earth (Matt. 6:10) assumes that His will is not being done. Where then is our hope? It remains in the reality that, regardless of what has happened, our Redeemer does truly live!

Isn't Suffering Ultimately for Our Best?

To look at this accurately, it is important to first differentiate between types of pain and suffering. To say that it is unjust that I should feel pain as I absentmindedly stick my hand on a hot stove would be to misunderstand the value of my nervous system to make me aware of danger and personal harm. Likewise, God is not afraid to make us uncomfortable in order to teach us and bring us closer to Him. There are times that the decisions I make for my children are very uncomfortable for them and, with regard to discipline, sometimes painful. We know that this is good parenting, because it steers our children toward that which is best for them.

Sin, deception, and pride can be so entrenched in our lives that God will use discomfort and difficulty to bring them to the light so we can be conformed to the image of His Son, Jesus. In the C.S. Lewis book *The Voyage of the Dawn Treader* from his Chronicles of Narnia series, the boy named Eustace has turned into a dragon after horrible and selfish behavior. Aslan instructs Eustace that he must let him peel the scales off of him if he is to be cleansed and free. What then happens is that the boy is put through excruciating pain and discomfort as the great lion tears the scales off with his own claws. The boy feels pain but freedom at the same time.[2] I believe this is an accurate picture of how the Lord will take us through difficult circumstances to free us from our selfishness and rebellion.

Our ability to embrace these times with humility releases true freedom in our lives, yet to say that all pain and suffering invading our world is necessary reduces God's governing ability to something less than glorifying. It neither speaks highly of His character or ability to secure His will. I would like to suggest that this kind of thinking could alienate God from our grieving world while alienating us from understanding His passion to bring redemption.

Aren't We Told to Rejoice and Not Complain When Bad Things Happen?

There are many references in the epistles of Paul in which he glories in his sufferings and several encouragements from the letters of Peter that we should do the same. We are called to share in the sufferings of Jesus. The Scriptures even tell us to rejoice when this happens.

> Dear friends, do not be surprised at the painful trial you are suffering, as though something strange were happening to you. But rejoice that you participate in the sufferings of Christ, so that you may be overjoyed when his glory is revealed.
>
> —1 Peter 4:12–13

It must be noted that Peter was specifically addressing the persecution that the church was experiencing. (See 1 Peter 3:14–23; 4:1, 15–16.) Likewise, the references from Paul concerning suffering address specific persecution that he was enduring for sharing the gospel. Jesus Himself told us this would happen and to rejoice. (See Matthew 5:10–12; John 15:20.) Peter even says that these trials have come so that your faith may be proved genuine and result in praise, glory, and honor when Jesus is revealed. (See 1 Peter 1:6–7.) Persecution provides the opportunity to give witness of the hope that we have in Christ. (See 1 Peter 3:15.) Our confidence in the goodness of God when others are persecuting us has convinced many of the truth that we profess. This is a great honor. Our ability to rejoice in this suffering comes from sharing in the Lord's heart for His world and being given the opportunity to love Him with our very lives. To experience persecution at any level is painful, and yet we are offered a unique intimacy with the Lord and an opportunity to give a powerful witness of God's truth to an unbelieving world. The scripture is right when it declares that the world is not worthy of these heroes of the faith. (See Hebrews

11:38.) Yet persecution represents a small percentage of the suffering our world endures.

Still, a further look at Scripture reveals not only how we should respond toward persecution but what our attitude should be toward suffering in general. How do we respond to scriptures that instruct us not to complain at life's difficulties? We are all aware of the stories of the children of Israel in the wilderness and the grief that they brought to God by their complaining. Philippians 2:14 says, "Do everything without complaining or arguing." For several months after Sherry died, I felt a certain guilt for being so hurt. Living as a missionary for many years, I had seen suffering and hardship in the lives of those I had met around the world as well as in my own city. My mind told me I should just be thankful for what I had because there are so many others who have suffered much more. Often we feel that the prolonged grief we experience is self-centered and selfish. This leads to the disturbing conclusion that God is dissatisfied with us and our lack of true spirituality. I would remind myself that after all, Jesus endured far more suffering than I had. "I haven't the right to feel the way I feel," I thought. This perspective can generate guilt for the grief that we feel and cause us to think that God is less concerned for what we are going through. This way of thinking alienates God from us in our grief and keeps us from seeing His commitment to us accurately.

Grief is different than a complaining spirit. Healthy grief is the recognition of true loss with the capacity to see God's presence in our sorrow. Complaining is grief with the absence of faith. It's the inability to see God's loving commitment to us and is rooted in unbelief. The exhortation in Philippians to not complain is preceded by the reality of verse 13, which says, "For it is God who works in you both to will and to do for His good pleasure" (NKJV). The reason we can live without complaining is that we are confident that God will respond to any circumstance and choose to act in us according to His good pleasure. It's the ability to grieve with hope, to feel loss with the confidence that we are not alone. If we feel guilt in our grief, then we are powerless to see God's presence in our sorrow and therefore unable to grieve with hope in our own lives, as well as for those who may be greatly suffering around us.

A HEALTHY LOOK AT SUFFERING

There are many types of pain and suffering in the world. It is important, though, that we are careful not to associate useless suffering and evil with the Lord. The overarching theme of Scripture is not what God is accomplishing by ordaining all that happens but what He is accomplishing by responding to all that happens with power and redemption.

Perhaps you have heard it said that God is causing everything for our good. People often quote Romans 8:28, which says:

> And we know that *all things work together for good* to them that love God, to them who are the called according to his purpose.
>
> —KJV, emphasis added

In nearly every English translation of the Bible there are footnotes to this verse presenting it in several different forms. Let me give you two other translations that present some of the main variations.

> And we know that *God causes all things to work together for good* to those who love God, to those who are called according to His purpose.
>
> —NAS, emphasis added

And we know that *in all things God works for the good* of those who love him, who have been called according to his purpose.

—NIV, emphasis added

The main differences are on what God's activity seems to be in regard to things that happen. I have placed these differences in *italics*. The passage that this verse is taken from is one of the most amazing scriptures of promise and destiny in the Bible. To get the full meaning you must read the surrounding scriptures. I believe the emphasis is not on the fact that God causes everything that happens but that in everything that happens, God is working to cause good to come out of it, for those who are in a love relationship with Him. It's because God has already purposed us (those who love Him and have been called according to His purposes) to be like Christ (vv. 29–30). If this is true, who can thwart His plan, because "God is for us" (vv. 31–32)? Not only that, but Christ was raised to life and is interceding for us (v. 34); and if Christ is on our side, who or what can separate us from His committed love (v. 35)? Verses 37–39 sum it all up:

No, in all these things we are more than conquerors through him who loved us. For I am convinced that neither death nor life, neither angels nor demons, neither the present nor the future, nor any powers, neither height nor depth, nor anything else in all creation, will be able to separate us from the love of God that is in Christ Jesus our Lord.

The powerful lesson is that no matter what happens or who is against us, we can be conquerors because God is on our side and He will work on our behalf. If, by enduring suffering, we should experience spiritual growth, must we conclude that our spiritual growth was brought about because of suffering, or was it because we have a God who is able to transform any circumstance into spiritual growth if we allow Him to? One places an aesthetic glory on suffering, the other, a glory to God Himself. Often we want God to be the one orchestrating our circumstances because of our need to be assured that He is in control during times of great insecurity. God does not need to manipulate every circumstance in our lives to be in control because He has the foresight, wisdom, and power to manage any circumstance toward His desired end. God is never out of control because nothing is too difficult for Him. (See Jeremiah 32:27.) God's control is not a static reality but a vibrant, living, responsive thing. It seems to me that the emphasis in Scripture is not on God's meticulous control of all that happens but on His goodness in our failure and His ability to redeem our world. We are not challenged to find the hidden good in evil but to trust a God who can exchange our evil for His good. This ability is limited only by our willingness to embrace what He can offer to us in our brokenness.

Does God need the evils of this world to reveal His goodness, or is it better to say that God is so good (and so *committed* to good) that even tragedy cannot constrain Him? We cannot fully understand all that is going on around us, but we can know with certainty that God's heart suffers with us. When you experienced the pains of broken relationships, injustice, and evil, God was not just standing watching you, nor worse yet, the one manipulating the circumstance. Instead, He felt it with you. In my tragedy, I felt that God was grieving with me—not because He was helpless or did not have the power to act in the situation, but a true grief because it was never what He intended for His creation to go through. I realized that it was never God's intent for Sherry to deteriorate before our eyes through cancer and be taken from us so prematurely, or that my kids should have to grow up without the intended presence of their loving mother. This was not God's dream for our lives.

How will we answer the hopeless cries of the nations who are experiencing great tragedy and overwhelming evils? Recently, an issue of *U.S. News and World Report* magazine featured the picture of a woman leaning over the dead body of her young son. He had died in the tsunami that killed over 250,000 people in South Asia. Her face captured one of the most vivid descriptions of grief I have ever seen. If you could have been there by her side, how would you have revealed God to her? Of all people, Christians should be able to see this for the tragedy that it truly is because we know the state of our fallen, broken world and the disruption that it has brought upon mankind. We cannot fully understand God's jealous commitment toward redemption in His world unless we first understand the loss that He feels over that which He envisioned for mankind.

A Command to Hate Evil

Recently, I was speaking at an inner-city church and I shared how we should hate evil because God hates evil. A woman came to me after the service and said that she had a problem with my message. She just could not believe that God could hate anything and that we, as Christians, should not feel hate either. God does hate sin, and He calls us to do the same. Psalm 97:10 says, "Let those who love the Lord hate evil." And Proverbs 8:13 says, "To fear the Lord is to hate evil." The Hebrew word for evil here is *ra*. It is a broad word encompassing such definitions as "adversity, affliction, calamity, harm, hurt, misery, and that which is morally wrong."

To hate evil is to hate what it does to God and His creation. It's to be so aware of the good in God's original design that to aid in or even witness any disruption of that state should cause us to mourn. In Romans 8:19–20, we see that all creation eagerly waits to be liberated from the frustration brought upon its original design by the will of man. We not only see the existence of evil through the actions of men, but we suffer the consequences of decay on our world, brought about through the fall of man in the beginning. This hatred of evil and its effect is what enables us to see God in the fullness of His beauty and, according to Proverbs 8:12–13, that ability is the beginning of wisdom. Genesis 1:31 says that "God saw all that he had made, and it was very good." As we saw in the story of Lazarus, the sorrow and indignation that Jesus felt when He observed the pain of those around Him was in direct relation to His perspective of how far we had fallen from the good that He had created. If we remove our ability to feel brokenness and indignation at our disrupted world, then we steal our ability to have the same passionate jealousy that God has to bring redemption into that which belongs to Him.

When we feel the need to interpret God as the author of all that happens, we can spend much of our time trying to make sense of His loving character in the face of horrific circumstances and run the risk of missing the true emphasis of Scripture—God's incredible commitment to respond to our loss with identification and redemption. God is able to identify with your suffering because He is as hurt and frustrated about it as you. He is ready and able to do something about it. I am suggesting that as we partner with God in our sorrow, then we become able to partner with Him in His sorrow. We both honor God and bring hope to the world by calling evil the true evil that it is and focusing on God's commitment and ability to bring redemption out of our broken world. As we move potentially toward greater suffering at the hands of a fallen and cruel world, may we be a generation who are "more than conquerors" because we are convinced that nothing can "separate us from the love of God in Christ Jesus our Lord" (Rom. 8:37, 39).

When I returned from the hospital the night of Sherry's death, Jordan and Joseph were already asleep. I was up most of the night trying to figure out how I was going to tell them in the morning that their mother was gone. The kids had seen Sherry taken to the hospital countless times. They did not expect this one to be any different. They also had celebrated the news with us just weeks before that it seemed Sherry was beating the cancer. Their cousins had arrived for Christmas, and they woke up ready for an exciting day with family. It's one of those memories that you wish could be erased from your mind. As the family waited in another room, I asked the kids to come into my room and closed the door. We sat on the bed, and I told them that their mother's body gave out and had died while they were asleep. Our daughter, Jordan, who was nine and very close to her mother, just looked at me with disbelief and said, "Mommy has died?" Joseph, who was six, said, "You mean Mommy is not coming home?" We sat together and cried for several minutes. Over the weeks and months that followed, we would talk about Mommy daily, what she must be doing in heaven, things we remembered she liked, and how much we missed her. I always tried to include God in our sadness and how He was sad with us. What has happened is that our family's loss of Sherry has become a part of our intimacy with the Lord rather than a hindrance to it.

Often we feel that God is waiting for us to somehow graduate from our grief, as if a true sign of maturity is that point at which we no longer feel pain at the destructive loss we experienced. Again, this idea originates from the notion that God does not feel the loss the way we do and is simply waiting for us to get His "perspective" on the matter. The reason we feel pain at the remembrance of the losses we have endured is because we still recognize the value of what has been lost. To graduate from that grief is to no longer feel the weight of value in what was lost. To say that God does not feel the grief over our broken and fallen lives is to say that God somehow does not feel that what has been lost (whether loved ones, stolen innocence, or wholeness) is really that valuable. I would suggest that our spiritual maturity is not measured by an ability to move on from our grief but rather our ability to carry our brokenness the way God does. It's the ability to both live with the reality of true loss coupled with an expectation and confidence on God's redemptive commitment to us. Unless we truly believe that God is a partner in our grief, then we will feel guilt over our seeming lack of spirituality and be robbed of a true expectation of God's jealous commitment to bring redemption to our world.

Have you felt alone in your grief? Have you recognized the loss that God feels over your situation? Stop and share your pain with God. Weep together over the loss that you have endured. Extreme loss creates disorientation and an inability to navigate our future with direction and stability.

Every man reaches for something to give anchorage through life's most devastating storms. We instinctively trust that which we feel understands and identifies with us the most. If we are unable to see God as the one who relates with us in our suffering, we will turn to powerless alternatives. For some that trust remains only on them, being the only one they think can truly understand their loss. Others have resorted to lesser gods who they feel can identify with their world. Yet others, felling utterly alone, live life without any resemblance of stability at all. As Christians we must have an expectation in our loss that causes us to look for God's redeeming nature. We cannot afford to take a passive role in just waiting for God to make some sense out of our tragedy. Nor can we simply focus on managing our grief with an attitude of survival. God wants to share in your grief. When we become intimate with God in our grief, we no longer find ourselves fighting for our own dreams but for the bigness of His. Can you see Jesus standing at the entrance to the tombs of your broken life? Can you see His tears? If the Lord catches our tears in jars of remembrance, then there must be an ocean in heaven that contains His. (See Psalm 56:8.)

Lord, thank you that I am not alone in my hurt, but You share my pain. I am aware, now more than ever, the wrongness of this fallen world. May every reminder of this sorrow bring to my heart a greater hatred toward sin and the effect it has had on You and Your creation. Open my eyes to Your broken heart and give me the power to partner with You in doing something about it.

CHAPTER 3

BROKEN DREAMS

*After the servant had lifted him up and carried him
to his mother, the boy sat on her lap until noon, and
then he died.... "Did I ask you for a son, my lord?" she
said. "Didn't I tell you, 'don't raise my hopes'?"*

—2 KINGS 4:20, 28—

HAVE YOU EVER been crushed in spirit, the feeling you get
when everything has gone wrong? It's the despair we feel
when the thief behind our loss has come and gone. Many
times we look on the wake of destruction in our lives and think it would
have been better if we had never trusted the Lord for those things in
the first place. For some, the long history of abuse, broken promises
from those we trusted, and horrible tragedy have compounded this
sense of disappointment, making it harder and harder to believe God
for great things. Perhaps one of the greatest challenges for those who
have experienced loss is an inability to commit to taking risk with
God. It's not a lack of desire but a fear that any commitment will just
end up in failed and broken expectations. If anything, this generation
has such a longing to see those relationships and callings in their lives
endure to the very end that they are in a sense immobilized to take a
step toward true commitment for fear that it would end in the same
disappointment they have grown accustomed to in their world.

Since Sherry's death, I have found myself approaching life at times with tentativeness, a slight hesitation where I once would have rushed in with vision and faith. It may be toward ministry or just life in general. When I honestly look back on my day, I often find that I have spent more time trying to secure what I have than launching out with the visionary faith I once enjoyed with the Lord. Perhaps devastating loss can do that to us. That's the terrible thing about loss. It continues to steal from us long after the devastating tragedy has occurred. In the end, what has been stolen through the years can actually outweigh the loss initially experienced.

The story that unfolds in 2 Kings 4:8–36 can give us great hope and principles of how to face our broken circumstances. The account is of a Shunammite woman who was supporting Elisha's ministry by providing a place for him to stay as he regularly traveled through her town. Elisha was so blessed by her ongoing faithfulness that he felt the desire to bless her in some way. He learned that she had no son and her husband was old. Elisha called the Shunammite woman to him and told her that by the same time next year she would have a son. You would think that the woman would be jumping up and down with excitement. But instead she replied, "No, my lord. Don't mislead your servant, O man of God!" (v. 16). To understand her response, we must look at what a son represented within the Hebrew culture of that day. To not bear a son was considered a shame and a curse. It meant that you had nothing to offer toward the story of God's faithfulness on the earth. You might as well have not been born because you had not left a lasting mark for God's glory. It meant, in modern terms, that your life was unfruitful in God's kingdom.

This woman wanted God's call on her life to succeed so badly that she was afraid to even get her hopes up after waiting so long. But Elisha made her that promise and, sure enough, within a year she was holding a son. The story turns a dark corner though, when after her son had grown some years, he came running to his father with a splitting headache and died within hours on his mother's lap. She didn't even tell her husband what happened but saddled her donkey and went to find Elisha. The first thing she said to him when she met him on the road was, "Didn't I tell you not to get my hopes up?" (See 2 Kings 4:28.)

During the four months that Sherry battled cancer, we felt led of the Lord to pray for the fulfillment of all the dreams and callings that God had given us for our family and ministry. We had been serving the Lord as full-time missionaries in Chicago for twelve years. We had gone through tough and challenging times, but had a long list of promises and visions that God had given us for our city and family. On countless nights as I drove back and forth to hospital visits, I would pray with tears and passion for Sherry's life and the part that she would play in these things. Though Sherry had lost about fifty pounds during that time and looked like a skeleton, we were told only two weeks before she died that she was beating the cancer; much of the cancer around her brain had disappeared and with just a few more weeks she may be in complete remission. She lasted only two weeks more before her body gave out.

I cannot put into words the devastation that I felt. I had prayed so much before her death, and now I could not pray at all. I would sit and try to pray and nothing would come. I thought that it would have been better if we had not gotten our hopes up at all. The morning before her funeral, I sat alone with the Lord unable to say anything, and I heard Him ask me why I had stopped praying for the callings and destiny on Sherry's life to be fulfilled. My response was, "But Lord, she has died. We lost!" I will never forget His response. He said, "Just because Sherry is now with Me does not mean that I do not intend to honor My promises and her life. Keep praying for what I told you to pray!"

Elisha wasted no time in answering the distress of the Shunammite woman. He sent his servant ahead with his staff to lie on the boy, but nothing happened. In verses 32–35 we get the account of what happened once Elisha arrived:

> When Elisha reached the house, there was the boy lying dead on the couch. He went in, shut the door on the two of them and prayed to the LORD. Then he got on the bed and lay upon the boy, mouth to mouth, eyes to eyes, hands to hands. As he stretched himself out upon him, the boy's body grew warm. Elisha turned away and walked back and forth in the room and then got on the bed and stretched out upon him once more. The boy sneezed seven times and opened his eyes.

This was an unusual miracle to be sure. It would be well to assume that the extreme detail of Elisha's methods were instructed by the Lord since the scripture notes that Elisha walked the room and prayed to the Lord first before He got on the boy. I would like to suggest that the way in which the Lord instructed Elisha to pray was significant. As with the life of Jesus, we see that God not only reveals Himself through the miracles performed but also through the manner in which they happen. I am also struck by the attitude of Elisha in this story. He was disturbed at what the woman was going through. Not only was she suffering the loss of a child, but the promise of God in relation to her fruitfulness had been attacked. Not only had a precious relationship died, but the dream that came with that relationship died as well. For me, it felt as though the dreams of ministry and fruitfulness with the Lord that Sherry and I shared had died along with her. As I had envisioned the call of God on my family through the years, it had always included Sherry. Now I could not see any of it. It's like waking to find that someone has not only stolen the treasures of your home but the clothes off your back as well. Has the call of God on your life suffered loss, frustration, or derailment because of others' actions, your own failures, or circumstances beyond your control? Consider for a moment the three things that the Lord told Elisha to do.

Mouth to Mouth

The first thing Elisha does is place his mouth to the boy's mouth. The Israelites had a practice of reciting the victories that God had done for them in the face of difficult situations. We must speak into our losses, the testimony of God's faithfulness. The Psalms are full of such declarations.

> In you our fathers put their trust; they trusted and you delivered them. They cried to you and were saved; in you they trusted and were not disappointed.
>
> —Psalm 22:4–5

> We have heard with our ears, O God; our fathers have told us what you did in their days, in days long ago. With your hand you drove out the nations and planted our fathers; you crushed the peoples and made our fathers flourish. It was not by their sword that they won the land, nor did their arm bring them victory; it was your right hand, your arm, and the light of your face, for you loved them.
>
> —Psalm 44:1–3

The Israelites knew that God was a God of covenant. It meant that when He set His mind to do something with His children, He did not turn back until it was done. Like the Israelites, we honor God by remembering the promises of God not only to us but also to His purposes for the church. The scripture says in Psalm 68:6 that "God sets the lonely in families." The New King James Version says, "God sets the solitary in families." The Hebrew word is *yachiyd*. It means "one who is alone, the only one, solitary." The emphasis is not on those who just feel lonely but those who are truly alone, who are disconnected. God gives us a family so we may have a heritage of faith, a history of promise. The generation that separates itself from history removes its connection to the testimony of God's covenants with His children. The one who knows not only the history of God's covenants to him individually but also to those who have gone before him is one whose quiver is full of promises to unleash upon his most difficult circumstances. Listen to how the psalmist now identifies himself with the history of the Israelites in the verses following what we have just read in Psalm 44.

> You are *my* King and *my* God, who decrees victories for Jacob. Through you *we* push back our enemies; through your name *we* trample our foes. *I* do not trust in *my* bow, *my* sword does not bring *me* victory; but you give *us* victory over *our* enemies, you put *our* adversaries to shame. In God *we* make *our* boast all day long, and *we* will praise your name forever.
> —Psalm 44:4–8, emphasis added

Not only must we declare God's commitment to His purposes in our lives, but we must allow Him to breathe a new song into our losses and struggles. Consider these passages from the Psalms.

> Look on me and answer, O LORD my God. Give light to my eyes, or I will sleep in death; my enemy will say, "I have overcome him," and my foes will rejoice when I fall. But I trust in your unfailing love; my heart rejoices in your salvation. I will sing to the LORD, for he has been good to me.
> —Psalm 13:3–6

> I waited patiently for the LORD; he turned to me and heard my cry. He lifted me out of the slimy pit, out of the mud and mire;

he set my feet on a rock and gave me a firm place to stand. He put a new song in my mouth, a hymn of praise to our God.

—Psalm 40:1–3

We honor and reveal God's greatness when we allow Him to give us a new testimony in the midst of our struggles, a testimony of His faithfulness and redemption. We are all challenged by stories of those who have seen God's overcoming grace while suffering great loss. Our songs of God's redemption bring strength and hope to others. Psalm 34:2–3 says, "My soul will boast in the LORD; let the afflicted hear and rejoice. Glorify the LORD with me; let us exalt his name together." I have found great encouragement by the story of Horatio Spafford, a young Christian lawyer of Chicago in the late 1800s. After the Chicago fire destroyed his business and assets and then the death of his four children in a shipwreck six months later, he wrote the hymn that has remained to this day, "When peace like a river attendeth my way, when sorrows like sea billows roll, whatever my lot, Thou hast taught me to say, 'It is well, it is well with my soul.'"

What song does the Lord want to give you in the midst of your pain and loss? I am not suggesting that we go about with a superficial, everything-is-okay praise on our lips. I believe that He will give you your very own song, expressed in your own unique way—one that will be a point of intimacy in your relationship with Him for all of eternity. Put your mouth to that situation in your life that threatens to steal your destiny and speak God's story of promise and faithfulness into it.

EYE TO EYE

The next thing that the Lord instructs Elisha to do is to place his eyes on the eyes of the boy. In order to see life and restoration come to those terrible losses in our lives, we need to see God clearly. I have heard it said that "if our circumstances change the face of God, then we don't know God, because He never changes!"

The Israelites gained great strength during difficult times from knowing who God was. Consider these two passages from Psalms and Proverbs:

> The LORD is a refuge for the oppressed, a stronghold in times of trouble. Those who know your name will trust in you, for you, LORD, have never forsaken those who seek you.
>
> —Psalm 9:9–10

> The name of the LORD is a strong tower; and the righteous run to it and are safe.
>
> —Proverbs 18:10

The names of God in Scripture represented His character and abilities. We see in Exodus 33 and 34 that Moses cries out to the Lord to not send him away until He had revealed Himself to him. The Lord replies by saying, "I will proclaim my name, the LORD, in your presence" (Exod. 33:19). He tells Moses to hide behind a rock because no man can look on the face of God and live. Then a little later it says that "the LORD came down in the cloud and stood there with him and proclaimed his name, the LORD" (Exod. 34:5). What follows is a declaration of God's character passing before Moses. As Proverbs 18:10 tells us, when we run to who we know God to be, we are safe. We must cling to God's character and nature in the midst of our most shaking times. I believe that it is our glory to declare who we know God to be even when we cannot see Him, as we will discuss in another chapter. But it is also the very thing that gives life to the call of God in our lives. When David was running from the attacks of Saul, he wrote Psalm 18. It says in verses 1–3:

> I love you, O LORD, my strength. The LORD is my rock, my fortress and my deliverer; my God is my rock, in whom I take refuge. He is my shield and the horn of my salvation, my

stronghold. I call to the Lord, who is worthy of praise, and I am saved from my enemies.

The writer of Hebrews states in Hebrews 6:18 that "it is impossible for God to lie." In other words, God is the most trustworthy being in the universe. He is always faithful to who He is. He never has a bad day in which He is just not quite Himself. The generation that seeks His face will be the generation that seeks to see God's true character revealed in the hardest, most difficult situations of our day. The eyes of faith are not dependent on circumstances but absolute reality, whether seen clearly or not. God's nature and character are the only absolute, unchanging realities there are. Have you spoken those realities into your broken world? In Isaiah 50:10 we read:

> Who among you fears the Lord and obeys the word of his servant? Let him who walks in the dark, who has no light, trust in the name of the Lord and rely on his God.

This challenge is given to those who fear the Lord. In times where we seem to have no light and walk without the ability to perceive what is going on in our world, we must trust and rely on the name of God, who we know Him to be. Psalm 46:1–3 declares:

> God is our refuge and strength, an ever-present help in trouble. Therefore we will not fear, though the earth give way and the mountains fall into the sea, though its waters roar and foam and the mountains quake with their surging.

Throughout the Psalms, there is constant reference to tempests, storms, raging seas, and roaring waters. These are symbolic of those forces of chaos that we cannot control in our lives. But in all of these references, God is represented as the one who is unshaken and who is enthroned over the storm. Psalm 29:10–11 says:

The Lord sits enthroned over the flood; the Lord is enthroned as king forever. The Lord gives strength to his people; the Lord blesses His people with peace.

The word for "peace" is the Hebrew word *shalom*. It is a word that suggests wholeness in our being, having all things in order, being at rest in every area of our lives. I believe that we honor God greatly when we cling to His unfaltering character in the midst of our pain and suffering and allow Him to invade our world with wholeness, rest, and life. Is the call of God in your life suffering? Give it back its sight!

Hands to Hands

The last thing that Elisha does is put his hands on the boy's hands. Our hands represent fruitfulness. It's what we do for the Lord. It's the mark we leave on His world. We must understand that God is more committed to our fruitfulness than we are. John 15:16 states, "You did not choose me, but I chose you and appointed you to go and bear fruit—fruit that will last." God has destined us to be fruitful for His kingdom. To not fulfill God's call on our lives is a point of shame. But God does not want anyone to have shame in His presence. Psalm 25:1–3 says:

To you, O Lord, I will lift up my soul; in you I trust, O my God. Do not let me be put to shame, nor let my enemies triumph over me. No one whose hope is in you will ever be put to shame, but they will be put to shame who are treacherous without excuse.

I have come to believe that the enemy robs from us temporarily in hopes that he might rob something from God for eternity. For those who have put their hope in God, our losses are temporary. Some day our God shall restore all things. But the enemy's goal is not to merely disrupt our lives but to steal what could bring God glory for all of eternity, our fruitfulness.

Several months after Sherry died, my son, out of the blue, gave me one of those revelations that come to children so easily. He had been looking out the window of the car, which usually means that his mind is working, and he turned to me with these words of wisdom. He said, "You know, Dad, the devil can never win against God because God is stronger. There is really only one way that he can win and that's if he gets us to stop loving God." A few moments later he looked back at me and said, "But that will never work with us, because we are going to love God no matter what, right Dad?" I believe that God gave my seven year old an understanding of how to overcome the tragic loss of his mother with honor. We simply keep loving God.

Do the pains of your past threaten to rob you of your fruitfulness? This is why I believe that God told me to keep praying after Sherry's death for the fruitfulness that He intended from her life and the lives of my family. God is not only committed to His purposes through you, but He is committed to your honor. It's not because we deserve it or have the capacity to give Him anything of worth on our own, but because He is a giver by nature. We must continue to cry out to God for our fruitfulness. You can be certain that it is one of those prayers that He intends to answer. But we will not find that release unless we seek Him for it. Psalm 18:32–35 reminds us of God's commitment to us:

> It is God who arms me with strength and makes my way perfect. He makes my feet like the feet of a deer; he enables me to stand on the heights. He trains my hands for battle; my arms can bend a bow of bronze. You give me your shield of

victory, and your right hand sustains me; you stoop down to make me great.

God "stoops down to make [us] great"! Cry to the Lord for your fruitfulness. Our ability to be persistent with God in prayer is always to the degree that we are confident we are asking for that which He desires. We can know for sure that it is God's plan that we finish well. To say that tragedy, injustice, and evil could hinder God from fulfilling our destiny of intimate service to Him would be to lessen His glory as the Almighty redeeming God that He is. We must put our hands on the hands of our broken world and call out its fruitfulness once again.

Interestingly, after Elisha finished what God had told him to do, the boy's body grew warm but did not rise. The scripture says that after Elisha got up and walked and prayed around the room, he got back on the boy and did the same thing. Then the boy coughed seven times and opened his eyes. The boy did not rise the first time. It took more than one application of what the Lord had told Elisha to do.

Often, we must consistently address our losses and call their destiny back if we are to see life come into them. We will not have the ability to persevere in asking the Lord for our redemption unless we are able to see the jealous commitment the Lord has to those things that have been stolen. God does not want our lives to be riddled with fear and tentativeness. His desire is to restore our eyes of faith and expectation on Him, enabling us to continue the adventurous life of joyous risk to which He has called each of us.

In a later chapter we are going to look more closely at our fruitfulness and the things that threaten it. But as we consider the story we have looked at in 2 Kings 4, I want to encourage you with a scripture in Psalm 24:7–10. It reads:

Lift up your heads, O you gates; be lifted up you ancient doors, that the King of glory may come in. Who is this King of glory? The LORD strong and mighty, the LORD mighty in battle. Lift up your heads, O you gates; lift them up you ancient doors, that the King of glory may come in. Who is he, this King of glory? The LORD Almighty—he is the King of glory.

Our gates represent places of authority, confidence, and strength. Do you have ancient doors and gates that have been crushed and broken down, or shattered dreams of serving God with wholeness, confidence, and authority? Has your broken world left you feeling immobilized? Let the King of glory come into those ancient gates! Let Him give you a new song, not one that ignores your history but rather integrates His redemption into it. Let Him give you sight again, the ability to see His unshakable character; and let Him not only restore your fruitfulness, but multiply it for His glory.

Lord, there are times when I feel as if all the dreams that You have given me for Your glory have been shattered and have died. But I remember who You are, Lord, and what You have done with Your people throughout history. You are a God of faithfulness and covenant. You always keep Your promises. You have not changed. I am reminded of Your character, which is good, loving, and strong on behalf of those who put their trust in you. I will trust You, Lord. I will not let these circumstances rob You of Your right to reveal Yourself. Thank You, Lord, that You stoop down to make me great! I will wait for Your fruitfulness to be released in my life. It is You who have purposed to make me fruitful for Your kingdom. I will put my hope in You; let me not be put to shame.

CHAPTER 4

UNDERSTANDING REDEMPTION

The people of Israel are oppressed, and the people of Judah
as well. All their captors hold them fast, refusing to let
them go. Yet their Redeemer is strong; the LORD Almighty
is his name. He will vigorously defend their cause.

—JEREMIAH 50:33–34—

You, O LORD, are our Father, our Redeemer
from of old is your name.

—ISAIAH 63:16—

O NE OF THE overarching themes of Scripture is the idea of
God as our Redeemer. Yet the concept of redemption is not
common in our modern culture. It is a word that we use in
our worship and Christian phraseology, but, for many, it is one that has
lost its meaning. God has chosen to reveal Himself numerous times
in Scripture as a Redeemer. The prophet Jeremiah reminds us that
because God is a Redeemer, He will "vigorously defend [our] cause."
The prophet Isaiah declares that God's very name is "our Redeemer
from of old." It is a part of His character and the way in which He
approaches our circumstances. The very meaning of a redeemer is
defined by the way one responds to loss. It means that God is moti-
vated to respond to our struggles. In nearly every scriptural reference

to God being a redeemer, it is coupled with a statement of Him being almighty. God is not only a responder but is never at a loss for what to do. He is always capable of securing His end, no matter what is thrown our way. As we face the brokenness of our world and the overwhelming reality of loss around us, it is God's redemptive nature that gives us hope.

The 1828 Webster's American Dictionary gives this definition for the verb *redeem*: "to repurchase what has been sold; to regain possession of a thing alienated, by repaying the value of it to the possessor."[1] Because of loss, injustice, destruction, or sin, we have been alienated from those things that God has purposed for our lives. It is God's agenda to buy back our destiny, fruitfulness, and honor. When we encounter devastating loss, these things are threatened and we experience an alienation from the God-intended story for our lives. Another may have caused the brokenness and loss that we suffer, or it may be the consequence of our own sin and selfishness. But our hope lies in the reality that God is committed to removing our shame and buying back what has been stolen.

There was a constant feeling of ambiguity and confusion that haunted me after Sherry died. Our lives are like canvases. Every day brings another stroke toward God's intended masterpiece for our lives. One of the elements of our intimacy with the Lord is in sharing the discovery of that painting as it unfolds. Yet extreme loss is like throwing globs of paint over all the thoughtful and beautiful scenery of our life's canvas. My picture was not only no longer beautiful, but it had become unrecognizable. What had started out to become a masterpiece intended for display now looked like a mistake that could not be repaired. The worst kind of vandalism is that which destroys a beauty that cannot be replaced. I could not see how the story that God had set out to write through my family could be completed. The beautiful story of God in our lives can suffer the vandalism of loss and tragedy. For some, the canvas of our life was marred at such an early age that we never saw its intended beauty. For others, we tasted God's beauty on our lives, only to watch it smeared and become unrecognizable. In either case, we have become alienated from our intended glory and the honor of displaying God's story of beauty and magnificence. The God of the Bible is a God who jealously desires to buy back that which our broken world has vandalized.

The feeling of alienation from the intended glory that our hearts tell us we were made for can lead to a sense of despondency. We find ourselves just walking the shattered streets of our past, looking for home but never really finding the home we once had. If we spend all our time trying to understand why God may have done these things to us or resign ourselves to our perceived duty of thankfully accepting everything that comes our way, we can lose our focus on God's commitment to redemption in our lives.

The story of the Bible is a story of redemption. Jesus is revealed as both the fulfillment of that expected hope and the beginning of its implementation. Scripture reveals that Jesus came for three distinct objects of redemption.

1. What belongs to God

Jesus sought to buy back what had been stolen from God. (See John 17:1, 25–26; 2 Corinthians 5:18–19.) Revelation 5:9 declares that the Lamb has "purchased men *for* God from every tribe and language and people and nation" (emphasis added). Though we enjoy the benefit of a restored relationship with our Creator, we are being given back to God. When sin entered the world, it was not only man who experienced alienation from that which we were created for, but God also experienced alienation from that which He both created and deserved the enjoyment of. Jesus repeatedly revealed that the motivation for all that He did was to bring glory to the Father. We find comfort in John 3:16 because it reveals that God so loved the world that He gave His

Son for us. It could be said that Jesus so loved the Father that He gave His life to buy back what had been stolen from Him.

2. Our intended place with God

Romans 3:23 declares that all have "[fallen] short of the glory of God." One of Jesus' redemptive purposes is to buy back our intended glory, that place of beauty that sin and its effect on our world have stolen. John 17:3 reveals that we were made for relationship with God. The sacrifice of Jesus restores that possibility. Loss and brokenness threatens the destiny we all share. The passion of Jesus is not merely to secure for us a place in heaven but to return to us the amazing wonder of our existence—the ability to walk in a loving friendship with our maker.

3. Our intended gifts to God

In Revelation 5:10 we see a picture of what Jesus bought back for us. The verse says that He has made them to be a kingdom and a priest unto their God. Jesus has redeemed the honor of our existence—to minister to God's heart and serve His kingdom dreams. Most Christians are aware of redemption as it relates to our salvation and intended place with God. Fewer understand what Jesus sought to buy back for the Father. I am suggesting that fewer still understand that Jesus went to great lengths to buy back our honor—that ability to finish writing a story of God's greatness through our lives. It is this redemptive agenda for which we must ask the Lord to give us a fresh revelation. Unless we understand God's jealous desire to give us back the destiny we have—to live with fruitfulness and purpose—we can be tempted to just survive our losses and simply wait for the joy of our eternal home. Yet in doing so we sacrifice so much that the Lord was not willing to concede.

Because God is a redeemer, He approaches our losses with all three of these passions. We must approach our losses with the same. The

Israelites reminded themselves that God was a redeemer in the midst of all their troubles.

> They remembered that God was their Rock, that God Most High was their Redeemer.
>
> —Psalm 78:35

> For your Maker is your husband—the LORD Almighty is his name—the Holy One of Israel is your Redeemer; he is called the God of all the earth.
>
> —Isaiah 54:5

> Rise up and help us; redeem us because of your unfailing love.
>
> —Psalm 44:26

We too must remind ourselves often of the redemptive commitment of our God. By doing so, we learn to expect Him to act in our losses. When we expect Him to act, then we are challenged in our own lives to not resign to despair but to fight for the destiny that God has purposed for us. God is jealous over our redemption. He surely paid a great price for it. I have come to believe that it is actually His right of honor to have that place in our lives.

A STORY OF REDEMPTION

The Book of Ruth reveals the importance of redemption in an amazing way. The fact that an entire book of the Bible is committed to this concept reveals God's desire for us to understand this aspect of His character. The story is about a family of Israelites during the time when judges ruled the Promised Land. Elimelech, with his wife, Naomi, and their two sons, went to live in the land of Moab for a while. After some time, the two sons married Moabite women. The story does not tell us how or when, but Elimelech, along with his two sons, died and left Naomi and her two daughters-in-law, Orpah and Ruth, as widows.

Naomi and her family had land in Israel. It meant that they had a place to contribute to God's story on the earth. But she and her daughters had lost that inheritance through the loss of their husbands. They had become alienated from their destiny. Naomi is overcome with despair and feels that God has abandoned her. But the story is about God's provision. Ruth discovers that there is a "kinsman-redeemer," someone connected to her family, who can buy back the land for Naomi and Ruth. Boaz in this story represents the place that God holds in our lives. Jesus is our Kinsman-Redeemer. He has the authority to buy back the destinies from which we have been alienated. Jesus has paid the price to have that place in our lives. It is His right to buy back that from which we have been alienated because of sin or loss. Jesus has given us back the honor of completing our intended stories with God. We must understand the jealousy that God feels over this place in our lives. Often we struggle with despair and hopelessness, not because of a lack of faith in God's ability but a lack of confidence that God will act on our behalf. God sees it as His right to respond in our loss and brokenness.

Are you expecting God to move in your life? When you revisit the pain of your world, does it cause you to run to your Redeemer and cry out for redemption? The tragic losses we experience threaten our ability to complete God's call on our lives with fruitfulness and honor. Over the months after Sherry died, I not only grieved her absence but felt that my ability to continue in a life of purpose and fruitfulness for the Lord had been challenged. I felt an increasing alienation from the dreams that God had once given my family to live life to the fullest for His glory. God not only wants to comfort us in our grief but also desires to buy back our intended destinies. Isaiah 61:8 states: "For I, the LORD, love justice; I hate robbery and iniquity." God despises the thievery of loss and suffering in our lives. He wants to remove your shame. It is His right of position in your life. He is held back only by our lack of expectation on Him. We have become too accustomed to covenanting with our shame rather than with our Redeemer.

After the discovery of a kinsman-redeemer, Ruth displays great boldness before Boaz. Under Naomi's instruction, she waits until Boaz has fallen asleep. Then she uncovers his feet and lies down beneath them. When Boaz awakens and sees Ruth, she appeals to him and says, "I am your servant Ruth. Spread the corner of your garment over me since you are a kinsman-redeemer" (Ruth 3:9). This action would symbolize that Boaz had chosen to covenant himself with Ruth and cover the shame of her alienation. It meant he was willing to marry her. Jesus not only extends His authority to us for our destinies, but He desires to covenant Himself with us and cover our shame with His care. He will marry us, promising that He will finish His story with us. We need to approach God with boldness and appeal to His right to be our Redeemer. We will find the courage to lie at His feet in our brokenness to the degree that we see His passionate desire to have this place in our lives.

Stop for a moment and ponder the eagerness of your Maker to respond in the difficult circumstances of your world. The enemy tries so very hard to convince us that God is disinterested in what we are going through, unable to act, or worse still, that He is the one causing all the evil that we see around us. Each of these conclusions steals our ability to see Him as the one who, as Jeremiah said, is committed to "vigorously defend [our] cause" (Jer. 50:34). He is ready to act! He is capable of succeeding on our behalf! He is the defender of our honor and the remover of our shame!

Extreme loss has a way of identifying us with others who suffer the pains of this fallen world. Ever since I lost my wife, I find myself overcome with the suffering I see in others. At the same time, something else wells up inside of me—a strong desire to see redemption in their lives. I have become intimately acquainted with this aspect of God's heart. I have become extremely aware of God's jealous desire over the redemption of His creation. I now have a great expectation of God's willingness to remove this generation's shame and buy back its honor. Can you feel that expectation in your life? Do you have a growing expectation of what God is ready to do in your circumstances? In another chapter, I have stated that the great losses of this generation provide a unique opportunity for us to defend the name of our God. I also believe that it has created an opportunity for God to show His great commitment toward redemption, displaying His power in ways that no generation has ever experienced before. Ruth became the great-grandmother of David and eventually part of the very lineage of Jesus. When God redeems our lives, He not only puts our destiny back on track, but He also often shows His overwhelming commitment to us by creating a greater honor in our lives. The story of Ruth can be our story.

Redeeming Job

The end of the book of Job reveals a great picture of God's redemptive commitment in our lives. God gives Job several new children and greater prosperity than he had before. Honestly, I used to struggle with this passage of Scripture, especially after my wife died. You see, for those who have lost loved ones, no matter how grand new relationships or new children that come into your life may be, they cannot replace the significance of those relationships that were lost. Often I have heard people refer to the end of Job's story as a way of saying, "See, it's all right what you are going through; God will make it up to you. He made it better for Job, didn't He?" Somehow I think we are missing something by interpreting it this way.

God is a God of continuity, and we who are made in His image reflect this same characteristic. Our relationships, experiences, and memories adorn us as much as our physical features. If God were to erase everything and just start over, it would be like looking in the mirror at someone you have never known. The experience would not be a blessing but a loss of grave proportions. When God gave Job new children and prosperity, it was not to say, "That's all right, Job. See, I'll just start over and give you a new story. I'll even make it better than the last." To do so would not only devalue the entirety of Job's life up to that time, but it would also ignore the abrupt interruption to Job's story and the significant stories of those who had been lost.

I would like to suggest that the blessings the Lord brought to Job at the end of his life were not to replace his previous blessings, nor to somehow recompense Job for the supposed wrong that God had done to him. Rather, it was to reveal God's commitment to Job's redemption. What God did in that act was to give Job back the honor of his fruitfulness. It was to say to Job, "Your story is not over!"

> The LORD blessed the latter part of Job's life more than the first. He had fourteen thousand sheep, six thousand camels, a thousand yoke of oxen and a thousand donkeys. And he also had seven sons and three daughters.... After this, Job lived a hundred and forty years; he saw his children and their children to the fourth generation. And so he died, old and full of years.
>
> — Job 42:12–13, 16–17

After the great tragedy of loss in Job's life, his wife urges him to just curse God and die. Have you ever wondered why Satan destroyed every other member of Job's family but left his wife? His plan was to use the wife to speak doubt and accusation against God's faithfulness. The wife's encouragement was, "You might as well just die,

Job, because there is no more reason to live. God has abandoned you. You no longer have any hope or purpose to your life." (See Job 2:9.) Job's refusal to believe that about God allowed God to write the final chapter. God was able to show His true character in Job's life.

What God did for Job could not have taken away the pain of losing his previous children, but rather it redeemed his honor and continuing place in the story of God's faithfulness. The emphasis put on the abundance of livestock reveals the place of power and authority that God gave back to Job. This meant that God was committed to give Job the resources he needed to finish the call of God on his life. The blessing of children and long life revealed God's commitment to give Job a lasting testimony, the honor of continuing the story of God's greatness through his family. God is committed to all of these things in our lives. No matter what you have suffered or may suffer in this broken world, God will defend your honor and ability to complete your contribution to His faithfulness throughout history.

WHAT MOVES GOD'S HEART?

Throughout Scripture, we find a few things that always evoke a response from God. In Luke 7:11–13, it says that Jesus was moved with "compassion" (KJV) when He came upon a widow who was mourning the loss of her only son. His compassion moved Him to raise her son to life. In Matthew 14:13–14, Jesus tries to go away to mourn the loss of His friend and cousin, John the Baptist, but when He saw the crowds gather in desperation at the seashore, the Scriptures say, "He had compassion on them." His response was that He healed their sick until nightfall. In Matthew 15:32, several thousand people had gathered around Jesus while eating nothing for three days. In desperation for a touch from Jesus they had stayed, regardless of their hunger. Jesus, being concerned about their strength, said to His disciples, "I have compassion for these people," and miraculously fed them all with a few fish and loaves of bread. In Matthew 20:29–34, Jesus has "compassion" for the desperate cries of two blind men. In Matthew 18:23–27, it's the plea of one asking for mercy that moved Him toward "compassion" (KJV).

In all of these references the word translated as *compassion* literally means "to have the bowels yearn," in other words, "to make the stomach sick with longing." When God sees the suffering of our fallen world, there is a yearning from the depths of His being for our redemption. The heart of God reacts to our brokenness. The Almighty is moved by our losses, whether self-imposed or brought about by circumstances beyond our control. We can assume that there were those in the region of Jesus' ministry that did not experience His redemptive touch. Why these people? Isaiah 57:15 gives us a glimpse into what moves God:

> For this is what the high and lofty One says—he who lives forever, whose name is holy: "I live in a high and holy place, but also with him who is contrite and lowly in spirit, to revive the spirit of the lowly and to revive the heart of the contrite."

God declares that He not only lives in a high and holy place but also with those who are contrite of heart and lowly in spirit. The word *contrite* literally means in Hebrew "crushed like powder" and the word *lowly* means "depressed, brought low."

Has the suffering of your world left your heart feeling "crushed like powder" or has loss left your spirit "depressed" and in the depths? God's desire is to revive the spirit and heart of those who have been devastated by loss. God specifically makes His home in our brokenness. There were times when I found myself late into the night unable to sleep because my heart felt like powder. When all is as it should be in our world, we have focus and the ability to see our destinies with faith and confidence. But my broken world left me feeling like a river without banks. My life felt out of control, messy, and I was unable to anticipate where I was going. Yet during those times, unable to even cry out to the Lord, I would somehow sense His presence all around me. Not only did I feel His presence, but I would also sense a deep longing on God's heart to respond to my loss, a jealousy to defend and revive me.

I have met people who have suffered great loss but have not experienced that presence of the Lord or realization of His yearning to respond. I am suggesting that it is not because God is not there, but because we have lost our expectation of Him to make His dwelling in our brokenness. When we lose the revelation of God's overwhelming desire for redemption in our lives, we lose our ability to anticipate His response and therefore often remain helpless in our suffering. We need to build highways into our lives for the Lord's compassion and give Him the honor of responding with jealousy over all that has been stolen.

God has actually given us an authority in our losses to claim His redemption. First John 5:14–15 says, "This is the confidence we have in approaching God: that if we ask anything according to his will, he hears us. And if we know that he hears us—whatever we ask—we know that we have what we asked of him." Our understanding of who God is and that His will is to buy back that which we have been alienated from gives us a confidence to approach Him with cries for redemption. Because it is God's jealous will to be a redeemer in our lives, we have the authority to ask Him for it. Perhaps this is what threatens the enemy's goal of destruction in our lives the most. He knows that if we recognize the authority we have to invite God's redemption in our losses, we may release God's power in our lives like we have never seen before. It's for this reason I believe the enemy seeks to keep our eyes off of God's redeeming commitment in our losses and convince us that it's our religious duty to simply accept all that comes our way.

The message of God's redeeming nature is a message for our time. As we struggle and relive the losses of our lives, God desires to be our Redeemer. As a generation marked by suffering and the destruction of life, we must expect and cry out for the redemption of our place in history. This generation has the authority to unleash God's glory on the earth by crying out for redemption in its overwhelming loss and brokenness. A world overwhelmed by tragedy must be encouraged to see the redemptive commitment of our God. The enemy's only chance for victory is to get us to give up and stop expecting God to redeem. The generation that refuses to let go of God's redeeming nature is a generation positioned for power, authority, and honor! May the Lord give us eyes to see the jealousy His heart holds over our redemption.

Lord, I am so grateful for Your loving commitment to my redemption. Please come and take that place of honor that You deserve in my circumstances. I refuse to resign my life or give in to the lies of the enemy. You are a faithful God. I know that You are more committed to defending my cause than I am. I long for Your redemption in my life, the lives of my family, and of my generation. I give You thanks because I know that You are faithful and good. You are both able and ready to redeem us. Come and write the final chapters of our lives, so the world may see You for the faithful God that You are.

CHAPTER 5

FINDING RESTORATION

Be at rest once more, O my soul, for the
Lord has been good to you.

—PSALM 116:7—

The Lord is my shepherd.... he restores my soul.

—PSALM 23:1, 3—

IN THE PREVIOUS chapter we considered the Lord's passionate commitment to our redemption. If redemption is the buying back of our unique place in God's story on the earth, then restoration is the returning of all that we need to continue in that story. When we face tragedy, injustice, and difficult circumstances, we can lose much that once gave us strength and confidence. After Sherry died, I became painfully aware of that loss. Sometimes I found it hard to function. I felt as if half of me was gone. I found myself asking God, "Who am I?" I simply did not feel like the same person. There were times when I would look in the mirror and feel as if there was someone else looking back at me. The person in the mirror looked broken, damaged, and somehow no longer whole.

God is not only committed to redeeming our honor and His intended purpose for our lives, but He is also committed to restoring our souls. He has promised to return to us the wholeness needed to finish the race to which He has called us.

David said in Psalm 23 that the Lord "restores" his soul. This same Hebrew word is translated as "returned" over a hundred times in Scripture. It means literally to return something back, to retrieve, or recover. In other words, David was declaring his confidence that the Lord would return back to his soul what was lacking. God would recover the wholeness of his innermost being. God has purposed each one of us to be vessels that can carry the fullness of His dreams for our lives. Our brokenness in this world threatens our ability to continue carrying those dreams. God's desire is to return to us all that we need to continue in the destiny that He has purposed for our lives.

THE YEAR OF THE LORD'S FAVOR

In Leviticus 25, we get a glimpse of God's commitment to restoration. He was communicating to the children of Israel instruction about the Year of Jubilee. Every fifty years anyone who had lost his or her family's allotted land was to have it returned. In verse 10 it states, "Each one of you is to return to his family property." Again, in verse 13 it says, "In this Year of Jubilee everyone is to return to his own property." In verses 25–28 there is specific reference to those who have lost their land through poverty or debt; it was to be returned to them. To capture the significance of this passage we must remember that to the Israelites, the possession of land meant that they played an important part in God's purposes for the nation. It represented the resources needed for fruitfulness and the opportunity to reveal God's faithfulness. To not have land meant that you were not contributing to God's redemptive purpose for Israel. God was committed to restoring those resources to anyone who had lost them through the struggles of life. The emphasis is not just the external possession of land, but also the possession of that which would provide for fruitfulness. This speaks of God's loving commitment to us. He has not only honored us with a significant part to play in His story on the earth, but He has promised to return to us those resources needed to fulfill that destiny.

When David used this same Hebrew word in Psalm 23, I believe this was the kind of restoration he understood and expected from the Lord. God restores the soul. It is not the externals that release or hinder our fruitfulness, but our internal stability. Numerous times in the Psalms, the children of Israel declared that it was the Lord who provided that internal stability no matter what was raging on around them. Psalm 46:1–3 says:

> God is our refuge and strength, an ever-present help in trouble. Therefore we will not fear, though the earth give way and the mountains fall into the heart of the sea, though its waters roar and foam and the mountains quake with their surging.

Interestingly, in Leviticus 25:9 we are told that this time of restoration was to take place on the Day of Atonement, the one day out of the year where the sins of the whole nation were atoned for by blood sacrifice. This was to remind us that the atonement of Jesus has provided for our restoration. Jesus paid the price, not only for our redemption but also for our restoration. In Luke 4:16–21, Jesus stood in the synagogue and quoted a scripture out of Isaiah. He then said to them, "Today this scripture is fulfilled in your hearing." Take a look at this passage in Isaiah 61:1–4.

> The Spirit of the Sovereign Lord is on me, because the Lord has anointed me to preach good news to the poor. He has sent me to bind up the brokenhearted, to proclaim freedom for the captives and release from darkness for the prisoners, to proclaim the year of the Lord's favor and the day of vengeance of our God, to comfort all who mourn, and provide for those who grieve in Zion—to bestow on them a crown of beauty

instead of ashes, the oil of gladness instead of mourning, and a garment of praise instead of a spirit of despair. They will be called oaks of righteousness, a planting of the LORD for the display of his splendor. They will rebuild the ancient ruins and restore the places long devastated; they will renew the ruined cities that have been devastated for generations.

Jesus came to fulfill God's commitment to our restoration. Notice in verse 3 what He promises to provide for His people. He will provide a "crown of beauty instead of ashes," "gladness instead of mourning," and "a garment of praise instead of a spirit of despair." This is God's response to our broken situations. He is a restorer. He will replace the ashes of your life with a crown of beauty. This speaks of the returning of your glory in place of the shame of your brokenness. He will restore to you gladness in response to the thief behind our losses. He promises to replace despair with praise. That means He will take away your sense of hopelessness. Job's wife was wrong to want to just curse God and die, as if there were no longer any reason to live. (See Job 2:9.) God had not abandoned them. God is the great Responder. He is never at a loss of how to return you to wholeness.

God has promised to respond to the ashes of our circumstances by adorning our lives with beauty. God's covenant promise to respond to our broken world is what gives us the authority to ask Him for it. We have the capacity to release God's powerful restoration in our tragic situations by approaching Him with the confidence of who He has revealed Himself to be in our brokenness. Unless we understand God's attitude toward our loss and jealous desire to restore what has been stolen, we will not take the authority He has given us to open the doors of our shattered lives to the fullness of His redeeming nature. Often we hold God back from bringing restoration in our lives by not recognizing His overwhelming commitment to us in the tragic losses of our fallen world.

Not only is God committed to our restoration, but Isaiah 61:3–4 reveals the intended result. Those whom God restores will be "a planting of the Lord for the display of his splendor." Just like God promised the children of Israel in Leviticus, the Lord will return to you your ability to display His splendor on the earth. Isaiah goes on to say that these restored individuals will "rebuild ancient ruins," "restore places long devastated," and "renew" the ruins from past generations. What a promise! The enemy would have us think that our world is so broken that we could not possibly have anything left to offer. Instead, God promises to return to us what we need to not just survive but to "restore," "rebuild," and "renew" God's dreams for our generation and even the losses of previous generations.

When you look in the mirror and see brokenness, remind yourself of God's commitment to you. Often we resign ourselves to simply trying to survive our losses when the Lord wants to reveal His restoring nature and return us to a place of destiny in His kingdom. Not only does God want to restore you, but there are millions of people who need to hear of God's true nature. They are living in ruined destinies, hungering for someone to help rebuild and renew their purpose for living.

FILLING THE VOID

When I was twelve years old, I was awakened in the middle of the night by my mother, who told me the news that my father had died in a terrible car accident. Over the next few days the slow realization that my father was gone began to sink in. I remember sitting outside the house one night asking the Lord why my father had died. When someone feels that the Lord has spoken to them, it is always hard to describe exactly what happened, but that night I knew that God was speaking to my heart. As I called out to the Lord, a scripture came to my mind that I remembered hearing in Sunday school. It was Psalm

68:5, which says that God is "a father to the fatherless." I immediately felt the Lord say that He would be my Father if I would ask Him. There was a deafening silence as I felt the Lord waiting for my response. That night I asked God to be my Father. I felt sure that God had responded to me. To this day, I still feel the loss of my dad, sometimes at the most unusual times. But from that day as a twelve year old to the present, I have been acutely aware of God as my Father. It was God who provided the reassuring approval I needed from my father over the years. It was God who was always there with wisdom, instruction, and provision. I miss my dad and look forward to seeing him again in heaven. But because of God's commitment to the void left in my life through the loss of my dad, I have never missed what I needed to be whole.

Global tragedy and personal loss have forced countless children to live life without the God-intended relationship of loving mothers and fathers. It is shallow and unrealistic to think that we should just get over these losses. As much as we would like to think otherwise, we do not simply move on from parental abandonment or the reality of a stolen loved one. God desires to fill that gaping hole. In 1991, I stood in front of twenty-five orphaned children in Romania, most of them abandoned by their parents. Few even remembered ever having a mother or father. I shared my story and told of how God took the place of my father over the years. I related to them God's overwhelming desire to provide the intimacy, comfort, and direction of their absent parents. We do not have to live our lives with a deficit. The loving and capable hands of our Father in heaven can restore all that we have lost in the most vulnerable part of our hearts. I am not suggesting that we simply embrace a cozy idea that God will just take all the pain or sense of loss from us. That again is too simplistic and ignores the extreme value of what has been lost. Rather, God is able to make a real transference of Himself at each and every point of need existing in our broken souls. God will become what we need to be whole. He provides that wholeness whenever the fangs of our devastating losses penetrate our emotions and memories.

Both of my children have expressed reoccurring sadness at the loss of their mother. Though my daughter chooses not to vocalize that loss often, I see it regularly in her eyes. She gets that look at moments when we both know that Sherry should have been there, those times when Jordan wants desperately to share a special moment, an exciting accomplishment, or just simply who she uniquely is with her mother. I can see that longing in her eyes to hear what her mother would say to her, a longing to be reassured in a way that only a mother can do. On the other hand, my son is extremely vocal in his thoughts and emotions. I always know when he is missing his mother. Like Jordan, it begins with an expression of sadness, but Joseph is not quite as confident in what to do with the pain and loss that he feels. On one such occasion when Joseph was just seven, he got that look on his face at some unique moment in which Sherry was remembered, and I asked him what was wrong. He quickly responded, "I miss Mommy so much, Dad. It feels like my heart is empty. I don't know how to fill it up again." I am always quick to tell my son that I feel that sadness as well and miss his mommy greatly. I then remind him that God has promised to fill that empty spot in his heart.

To *restore* means to restock the shelves of our heart. God will restock the stores in the storehouses of our soul and spirit. God is committed to filling the voids left in our lives through loss. It could be the loss of a relationship that was once committed to us, or the loss of strength and confidence that we once enjoyed before the thief of injustice, suffering, or sin robbed us. For some, we may not be able to remember a time when we felt whole, having always felt like great, big parts of us were missing. I have come to believe that the Lord is jealous over His right to fill these voids. He will be a husband to the widow or abandoned wife. He will be a father or mother to those who have either lost or been abused by a parent. He will be our closest friend, our hope during times of despair, our stability during impoverished emotions. What are you lacking in your soul? What promised land have you lost through the harsh circumstances of this broken world? God is committed to restoring your wholeness.

After my father died when I was twelve, there were many things that I never experienced through his absence. I had asked the Lord to fill that void and be a father to me, but over the years it became a discovery as to all that I had lost and needed restored. At every revelation it became another chance to invite that restoration. Rather than becoming threatened by the thought of having to live life without all that God intended for my soul, I could cry out to Him for help. Interestingly, one of the things that I missed the most over the years was the privilege of seeing my father's face. I felt robbed of the opportunity to see his expressions during important and vulnerable times. I always wanted to know how he would approve of my stature, accomplishments, friends, even the woman I fell in love with. Would the look on his face reveal that he was proud of me? Would it show satisfaction in the choices I made?

I discovered several years into my adult life that I had a deep fear of making decisions. It used to drive Sherry crazy. I struggled with a lack of confidence in whether I was making a good decision or not. I began to realize that the loss of being able to see my father's approval or disapproval over the years had left me directionless. A child looks to the face of his father to receive direction and understanding for his circumstances. It is the expression on a father's face that helps to give a child confidence in the decisions that he makes. It was one more way in which the losses of my broken world had left a void in my soul. Once discovered, it became another opportunity to invite the Lord to restore through His own character and presence, that which had been lost. I asked the Lord to provide that sense of direction that had been stolen from me through the loss of my father. God has allowed me to be so aware now of His face. I have discovered a new confidence and assurance in making decisions. This generation is experiencing a similar loss of direction and confidence through the brokenness of family relationships. These losses can be felt not only by those who have lost fathers, but by those who have suffered the relationship of an abusive or absent father.

What has caused the storehouse of your heart to be empty? God wants to restock the shelves of your innermost being. The message of hope to our world is a message of restoration. We can say like David, "The Lord restores my soul" (Ps. 23:3). What this generation needs is the revelation of how much is provided to them through the able and faithful hands of our heavenly Father. Man was made to be whole. We are designed to search out that wholeness. We will either find it in the restoring nature of our God or work in vain to some how hide the reality of our brokenness.

Looking Elsewhere

Though the Lord had revealed Himself to me in many ways through the losses of my childhood, the loss of my wife brought back that dark enemy of loss in far greater ways than I had experienced before. What do we do when that familiar feeling of pain, emptiness, and loss assails us? For many, it's not merely happiness that we seek, but escape. The chance to not feel anything may be more attractive than feelings themselves. We not only feel wounded by our world, but after this life has robbed us, it then demands us to just continue living. We are expected to go on and somehow just survive what this world throws at us. After Sherry died, there were many days that I felt numb and empty. I would be tempted sometimes to just go to sleep. I may have only been awake for a couple hours before I wanted to sleep again. It just sounded easier. At least while I slept I would not have to feel pain or the pressure to give out when I felt I had nothing to give.

Often, after time goes on, it's not only the tragic experiences we seek to forget but what we have become in response to our loss as well. Before Sherry died I enjoyed an ability to approach my world with patience, grace, optimism, and giving toward others. After her death, I disliked what came out of me. I was much more irritable. I yelled at my kids more. I seemed to look at things with cynicism. I had much less patience and struggled with a lot more anger. I felt more selfish and self-protective. I would find it hard to sleep at night some-times, simply because I felt the shame of how I had responded to my kids that day. The constant inability to pull something of value off the shelves of my heart to meet the daily demands of relationships and responsibilities overwhelmed me. I felt like a man going deeper and deeper into debt. I could not pull myself out of an ever increasing sense of shame. Maybe you have felt the same thing. I simply did not like what I had become. What do we do with these feelings of shame, brokenness, and emptiness? Life goes on and we are not only expected to continue living but we long to be able to finish what God has called us to without shame.

For some of us, we bury ourselves in fleeting experience, entertain-ment, or even food. These escapes are all attempts to hide the voids in our lives. Yet all the while the Lord is longing to restore us. Why is it that we no longer have the confidence that He is there for us in these times? Is it because we somehow feel it was He who produced this loss in our lives? Maybe we feel that we played some part in the devastation of our lives and believe God expects us to just accept our punishment. Perhaps we know that the Lord will restore us but feel this is something we must wait until eternity to enjoy. There is a resto-ration that will be given to us in eternity that will bring all things to complete wholeness once and for all. But I would like to suggest that

God is committed to a restoration in our lives here on Earth, not a restoration that removes all tears or even the difficult circumstances of this fallen world, but one that returns to us all that we need to joyfully fulfill his destiny on our lives. That restoration is for us whether we have caused our pain or someone else has.

The generation that will experience the fulfillment of God's desires is the one that allows God the only honor of filling the voids in their lives. The scripture in Psalm 24 later speaks of a generation that seeks the face of God. It is characterized by those who have a passion for purity, a commitment to defend truth, and an unwillingness to lift up their souls to an idol. We must not give our emotions, securities, or even our losses to anything other than the Lord. An idol is anything that holds a place of provision in our lives that belongs to God alone. It is the Lord who is committed to our restoration. We must become a generation that knows how to give God our losses and embrace His restoring nature in our lives. We do this by calling on the Lord in our times of despair and emptiness. When we feel the pains of our brokenness, we must cry out to God for that wholeness that He promises to give. It's not an easy transition for many of us. The world has trained us well in the art of escapism and counterfeit pleasures. We must be so aware of the restoring nature and commitment of our God that we find the faith to receive His provision for the moment. Every generation creates new ways to escape its loss and brokenness. Like the tolerance our bodies build toward drugs, demanding greater dosages to continue their effects, the previous generation's forms of escape no longer work for us. This leads to greater and more extreme forms of escapism, escalating until despair either leads us to a total mental and emotional shutdown or the most deceptive form of escape, suicide.

The promise of Psalms 24 is that the generation who seeks His face "will receive blessing from the Lord and vindication from God his Savior." Blessing speaks of provision, like what we saw in Isaiah

61:1–3. *Vindication* means that God will jealously defend our cause. The word is actually translated as "righteousness" in other passages. It means that God will reward those who seek His face alone with the righteousness He intended for our lives. He will fight for our intended honor and destiny before Him, like what we saw in Isaiah 61:4. We honor God by expecting this from Him.

Changing Our Identity

In the Book of Ruth, Naomi had become overwhelmed with hopelessness. After losing her husband and two sons, she returns to her homeland and tells her friends, "Don't call me Naomi....Call me Mara, because the Almighty has made my life very bitter" (1:20). The name *Naomi* means pleasant, but the name *Mara* means bitter. Her life went from being pleasant to experiencing a bitter existence. Nothing had appeal or joy any more.

Often we respond to the trauma of life a lot like Naomi. We are tempted to identify more with our loss than with our promised restoration. We begin to characterize ourselves through the lenses of our struggles. We can wear our loss as if it were a name written across our foreheads. We feel the need to introduce ourselves from the point of what we have lost, rather than from the destiny and calling that God is committed to continue in us. When asked questions like, What is the Lord doing in your life? we can answer with a phrase such as, "Well, I feel the Lord has called me to do this or that, but…" What follows are statements like, "Now that I am a widow…" or "Ever since my father died…" or "I was an abused child, so I have trouble…" or "I have dealt with poverty all my life, so it's difficult to…" Each of these traumatic situations are of great concern to the Lord, but we must look far enough into His compassionate face to see His jealousy over our destiny and eagerness to restore that which we need to fulfill it.

I have experienced many conversations with Christians who have allowed their losses to be barriers to God's abilities. To create boundaries in order to constrain us toward that which He has called us to do is honorable, but if we apply boundaries on God's call on our lives by limiting our ability to follow through in all that He may ask of us, then we are ignoring God's ability to restore us to fruitfulness. The world evaluates its options based on the resources at hand. As believers in an all-powerful, loving God who is committed to our restoration, we can look beyond ourselves to embrace His resources for our lives.

I discovered very quickly that to continue doing what God had called my family to do as a single parent was difficult, to say the least. Not only did it seem that the Lord was not releasing me from the burdens of ministry, but it looked as though He was increasing the load at times. I began to wonder what God must have been thinking. I wondered, "Doesn't He know that I am a single parent now? I am not the same person I was before. How can He expect the same from me?" I felt the Lord say to me that I could change my name if I wanted, but He had not. This was not based on a lack of sensitivity to my situation but rather an overwhelming confidence the Lord had in His ability to give me what I needed to be whole. When the familiar thief behind our loss comes and reminds us of what he has stolen, we must turn to who we know God to be and embrace His promise of restoration. We honor the Lord when we remind Him that He is the one who restores our soul. It is the nature of the world to define us by our circumstances and environment. It is the nature of God to define us based on His destiny for our lives. Regardless of what has happened to us, God's destiny for our lives has not changed.

The life of David provides a great example of this. In Psalm 139:16, David declares to the Lord, "All the days ordained for me were written in your book before one of them came to be." The emphasis of this scripture is not that God had purposed everything that had happened in David's life, but that God had already planned out the wonderful story of David's life before any day had come into being. It was not God's plan for David to commit adultery with Bathsheba or that he should murder her husband, Uriah. David had experienced as a child the trauma of a broken and abusive family. He was ridiculed and unloved by his first wife. He lost an infant son, and his eldest son, Absalom, betrayed him and tried to have him killed. As king he was taunted by his enemies and betrayed by his friends. It would be hard to conclude that the Lord ordained these things. Yet regardless of what David experienced, the Lord's plans for him had not changed. A glance at the Psalms reveals that David felt the confidence to bring these difficulties to the Lord. But rather than using these difficulties as an excuse to convince God that he could not finish the task, his expectation was on the Lord to provide for him what would be needed to finish what God had called him to.

God remains committed to restore us to his original destiny for our lives. When God speaks of David's life in Acts 13:22–23, He described him as a man after His own heart and one who fulfilled the Lord's purposes in his own generation. Not only did God fulfill His destiny for David's life in spite of all that he had experienced but also we have no indication that God ultimately identifies David with these losses or failures. Rather, he is identified by what the Lord had ordained for him. David understood that God had planned his life to be a certain way. It was this confidence that caused him to run to the Lord for restoration and help in times of trouble. You can run to the Lord with confidence. He will restore to you all that is needed to finish the race He has called you to. Hebrews 4:15–16 encourages us to run to the Lord in our weakness.

> For we do not have a high priest who is unable to sympathize with our weaknesses, but we have one who has been tempted in every way, just as we are—yet was without sin. Let us then

approach the throne of grace with confidence, so that we may receive mercy and find grace to help us in our time of need.

Now when I feel empty, as if parts of me are missing, and ask the Lord, "Who am I?" I hear Him say my name and remind me of the dreams and callings by which He has defined my life. It's as if the Lord says, "You are still the same person, Brad, and I am the one who will restore to you what your soul needs. Come; let's finish writing My story in you." We will fulfill our place in God's story through history to the degree that we allow Him the honor of returning to our soul beauty for ashes, gladness instead of mourning, and a garment of praise instead of a spirit of despair. (See Isaiah 61:3.) This is what Jesus purchased with His life. He deserves the right to fill the voids left in our lives through this fallen and broken world. May we find the courage to embrace this provision.

Lord, so often it feels as if there are great parts of me missing. I feel like I do not have what is needed to finish what You have asked of me. Yet I am confident that You are the one who restores my life. Return to me what my soul needs to honor You. I refuse to lift up my soul to an idol. You deserve the right to meet my deepest need. You are able to fill these voids in my life. I long to follow You wherever You may lead me. My soul will wait for You alone.

CHAPTER 6

THANKSGIVING FAITH

*Enter his gates with thanksgiving and his courts with
praise; give thanks to him and praise his name. For the
LORD is good and his love endures forever; his faithfulness continues through all generations.*

—PSALM 100:4–5—

IN THE WAKE of loss, injustice, and suffering, the doctrine of biblical thankfulness can be a difficult command to embrace. Why does God expect us to raise our eyes toward heaven with an attitude of thankfulness when what lies around us are the broken pieces of lost relationships, stolen innocence, and shattered dreams? Thankfulness is vitally important to the Christian life because it is inseparable from faith. Yet biblical thanksgiving is always portrayed as a response to our understanding of God. We approach our world with thanksgiving to the degree we are able to see our world with the eyes of faith. Therefore, if the focus of our faith is set on the wrong conclusions, our ability to walk in true thanksgiving will eventually erode.

Because my wife and I lived in full-time ministry for many years, my children have been exposed to Christianity their whole lives, and they have grown up hearing that God is good and that He should be praised in all circumstances. I began to notice a struggle in my six-year-old son several days after Sherry died. Every night, while saying his prayers, he felt the need to thank God in spite of his mother's death.

He would start off his prayers with, "Lord, even though Mommy died, I still thank you." He would then try as hard as he could to defend God and tell Him it was all right, even though he did not have a mommy any more. Yet, I noticed the struggle grow over the weeks that followed until he finally did not feel like praying before bed anymore, but just asked if I would pray instead.

Biblical thanksgiving is not a heroic resignation of desire where we learn to accept something of lesser value in the presence of something of greater worth. Rather, thankfulness is the ability to appreciate what has been provided for us in the midst of our circumstances, with the result of expecting more of that provision from the one who is good. As hard as my son tried to thank God for a life without Mommy, he knew in his heart that a life *with* Mommy would have been much better. Try as he might to defend what seemed to be God's expectation on him of accepting the loss of Mommy as a better thing than living with her, his faith in God's goodness slowly eroded. Rather than producing a greater expectation toward God's goodness, it was stealing his faith, causing a disinterest in continuing to pray for the future.

Not long after this struggle became evident, my son began to express his frustration while preparing for school one morning. He got that thoughtful look on his face and said, "I wish God did not want Mommy to be with Him so much." I asked him what he meant. He replied, "Well, if God didn't love Mommy so much, then He would not have wanted to take her to heaven so soon." Because Sherry had died on Christmas day, my kids had heard people say things to them such as, "Well, God must have wanted a special Christmas gift, so He took your mommy on Christmas;" or, "Your mom was so special that I guess God just couldn't wait any longer to have her with Him." Though these statements were well-meaning and given to comfort my kids, they were actually having an opposite effect. This idea began to paint a picture of God to my son that showed Him as less concerned for our needs and simply concerned only about His own. When we hold views like this about God and yet feel it is our duty to thank Him for our circumstances, then thanksgiving becomes a sacrifice and not a natural response of worship and trust.

I looked my son in the eyes and said very assuredly to him that God did not want to take his mother from him. I assured him that God was very sad that Sherry had died so soon and that he and Jordan would not be able to enjoy her as God had intended. I reminded him that Sherry's body was very sick and that though we cannot understand all the reasons why God chose not to heal her, it was a difficult decision for God to make. God wanted us to be together as a family; that was His plan for us. But since that plan had been broken, God wanted us to know that He promised to be there for us and provide whatever we need to get through this difficult time. I told him that he could expect God to always be very close to him because of the loss of his mother, and he could ask God for whatever he needed. I then added that because Mommy loved Jesus, we get an added blessing from God—to see Mommy again someday in heaven. Our discussion then led, as it usually did, to wondering what Mommy was doing in heaven and if she was helping Jesus decorate our future home there. It ended with Joe laughing about how Mommy was sure to remind Jesus how much he liked video games and to be sure and include that in his room.

Immediately Joe's prayer life changed. He wanted to pray at night more often. I love to listen to my kids' prayers because they reveal so much about what is truly going on inside. Joe's prayers became more reflective of a true faith and confidence he had in God's goodness. He found more things to be thankful for and always prayed with expectation of what God would do for us. Not long ago while getting into bed, Joe quickly declared that he wanted to pray first. He thanked God for the day that our family had together. It had been a fun family day, and we had been able to spend most of it just hanging out and playing as a family. He then made a very insightful statement. He thanked God for the day because it helped him not think so much about how he missed Mommy. I thought later how much that was a good description of grace. God provides what we need to endure through our pain and suffering. I am truly thankful that my God's faithfulness endures through all things.

Our ability to walk in true thanksgiving is based on the revelation of God's redeeming nature. As godly as it may seem, we do not honor God by thanking Him for all that comes our way, regardless of how evil or destructive it may have been. We honor God by thanking Him for who He is and who we know He will show Himself to be in response to the chaos and destruction that lies around us. God does not expect my son to accept the loss of his mother as something to be thankful for. Rather, God desires us to see His faithful commitment and care toward us in the midst of the true evils of our fallen world. By placing the emphasis of thanksgiving on our heroic ability to be happy with less than what we know would be the ideal for our lives, we lessen God's glory and glorify our ability to be self-effacing and self-sacrificing. This kind of religious thanksgiving makes heroes of people, when the true hero is who God is in response to our loss.

Psalm 100 reveals the foundational principals behind God-centered thanksgiving. These verses show us that biblical thanksgiving represents both a belief and an expectation. It's a belief that I am not an orphan and the expectation that God will faithfully father me in the future. Look at verses 1–3:

> Shout for joy to the LORD, all the earth. Worship the LORD with gladness; come before him with joyful songs. Know that the LORD is God. It is he who made us and we are his; we are his people, the sheep of his pasture.

We are commanded to worship the Lord with gladness because we know that He is God, He made us, and we are His people. It is the belief of whom we know Him to be and the reality that we belong to Him that enables us to face our broken world and declare with honesty that we are thankful. It's not our losses that we are to be thankful for but instead it is who He is for us and the position that He gives us as His children that evokes our worship and thanksgiving. This understanding does not war against my faith and confidence but fuels it. My losses have given me opportunity to understand what I am thankful for in God rather than steal my joy in His presence. The command of thankfulness is not a religious activity of self-sacrifice but an expectation on us to remember who our God is and that we are the people of His care.

When I began to understand what God truly expected of me through biblical thanksgiving, I experienced an incredible freedom and increase of faith. I was able to transfer my attention from my ability to accept my losses to the greatness of God and His commitment toward me. I found myself truly thankful because I belonged to the most loving, wise, and caring being in the universe. Rather than my loss challenging my ability to worship the Lord with honesty, I found a deep and natural response of worship rising up inside of me because of who I knew God to be in response to my loss.

Following our belief in who God is and the position He has given us in His heart is an expectation of what we know God will do on our behalf. Psalm 100:4–5 focuses our ability to be thankful on the realization of God's never ending faithfulness.

> Enter his gates with thanksgiving and his courts with praise; give thanks to him and praise his name. For the Lord is good and his love endures forever; his faithfulness continues throughout all generations.

Biblical thankfulness is built on an expectation that God's faithfulness will endure into the future. The word *endure* assumes that there are obstacles and stumbling blocks that must be overcome. God's faithfulness endures through all the obstacles that our broken and fallen world present. The eyes of true thankfulness are focused on God's redeeming nature and undying commitment to be faithful to us in spite of life's most difficult circumstances. The realization of great loss in my life has actually produced the opportunity for true thankfulness to take root. I have become overwhelmingly aware of my need for God's redemption, and because I have learned to expect that redemption, I find a natural response of thankfulness in my times with the Lord that is true and genuine. Scriptural thankfulness is always linked to the understanding and declaration of God's redeeming nature. If we seek to be a people who are truly thankful, we must take our attention off of our supposed duty of just being happy with what comes our way and place our eyes on the greatness of God and His commitment to me in my loss.

GIVE THANKS IN ALL THINGS

Often we are told that Scripture somehow commands us to be thankful for all that happens, as if there is some mysterious reason for our suffering that we just need to trust God with. Paul encouraged the Thessalonians to "give thanks in all circumstances, for this is God's will for you in Christ Jesus" (I Thess. 5:18). To the Colossians he wrote, "And whatever you do, whether in word or deed, do it all in the name of our Lord Jesus, giving thanks to God the Father through him" (Col. 3:17). To the Ephesians he declared, "Always [give] thanks to God the Father for everything, in the name of our Lord Jesus Christ" (Eph. 5:20). It would seem that Paul's common theme to the churches was to encourage them to maintain a heart of thanksgiving to the Lord.

I do not think the emphasis of these scriptures is on accepting everything that happens in our lives as something to thank God for. It's simply not consistent with the rest of what Paul writes in his letters to the churches. Most of the letters were, in fact, an admonishing response toward something the believers were doing wrong. Paul's attitude was surely not one of thanking God for the deception, sin, and false teachings that were finding their way into the churches. Jesus Himself showed frustration and displeasure toward the spiritual climate of His day, rebuking the Pharisees and Sadducees, even saying some of their activities were from Satan. We do not hear Jesus saying, "I thank you, God, for the deception of these religious leaders and how they have hurt and abused your children. I am sure that you have some good reason for it. Some day you will make sense of it all."

Rather, I would like to suggest that the reason we are commanded to thank God in all circumstances is because by doing so, we focus our faith on that which God can do in our lives no matter what happens. In other words, the emphasis is on declaring God as a redeemer who is capable of finishing what He has started, regardless of our hardships. We thank God because we are never alone. Our thankfulness declares to God that we believe He is a redeemer and committed to our cause. In Matthew 5:10–12, Jesus encourages us to rejoice when we are persecuted and abused for His sake. This is a matter of honor. When we endure persecution we are given opportunity to display our love to the Lord and His worthiness. But this is a small part of the suffering the world endures.

Often the world is frustrated at the church's acceptance of everything that happens. The nations long to see a God who is both compassionate toward their suffering and committed to responding to their sense of hopelessness. Our ability to thank God in all things is meant to be a witness of hope to the nations rather than a cold resignation to just accept our lot in life as some mystery of God's good will. Consider what these passages declare about the Lord through thanksgiving.

> You turned my wailing into dancing; you removed my sackcloth and clothed me with joy, that my heart may sing to you and not be silent. O LORD my God, I will give you thanks forever.
>
> —Psalm 30:11–12

> Give thanks to the LORD, for he is good; his love endures forever. Let the redeemed of the LORD say this—those he redeemed from the hand of the foe.
>
> —Psalm 107:1–2

> Let them give thanks to the LORD for his unfailing love and his wonderful deeds for men, for he satisfies the thirsty and fills the hungry with good things.
>
> —Psalm 107:8–9

If we place an expectation on people to "just be thankful for what happens even if you do not understand," we not only do God an injustice but we steal the very heart and witness of our true ability to be thankful. The result is that the church loses its relevance and is seen simply as a religious institution that is unable to address the true evils of suffering and devoid of true answers for a world overwhelmed with loss. The church's ability to experience true thankfulness is meant to bear witness to the world of what we know about God and our expectation on His enduring faithfulness. When we place our attention on the redeeming commitment of God, a hungering world experiencing great pain and loss will be drawn to Him.

GODLY CONTENTMENT

Another command of Scripture is contentment. Though it is linked to thankfulness, it more accurately represents a state of mind. Again, I am suggesting that there may be misconceptions on what biblical contentment is. First, we must understand what produces contentment. Like thankfulness, godly contentment was never intended to be a cold, religious duty but a response to an understanding about God. Paul said in Philippians 4:11–13 that he had "learned the secret of being content in any and every situation." The secret is revealed in verse 13 where he proclaims, "I can do everything through him who gives me strength." Paul was able to be content because he knew that God is the God of the possible; He is the great responder to any situation. Contentment is directly related to our ability to see God's redemptive and restoring nature. I can walk in contentment no matter what happens, not because I have found some super-spiritual ability to accept my brokenness as something good but because I am convinced of God's goodness in my brokenness. Again, the attention is on God, not me.

While thanksgiving is built on the ability to see what God has provided for me in my circumstances, biblical contentment is built on the expectation of God's goodness toward me in the future. It's a resting in who I know God will be for me no matter what may come my way. For anyone who has experienced loss and tragedy, this confidence in God is what enables you to continue to take risk, to be vulnerable, and to experience rest in the presence of future possible difficulties. I discovered not long ago how much this area had been threatened by the loss of Sherry in my family. One of the last things we did as a family before Sherry got cancer was the adoption of a cat for my daughter, Jordan, on her ninth birthday. Our entire family had gone to a cat shelter to look for the perfect family cat. Because my wife had a strong compulsion for justice and both my kids are extremely mercy-oriented, they chose the one cat out of a hundred who was so browbeaten and afraid that it would not come out of its cage. Sherry gave me that look that said, "We have to save this poor cat," and I knew the decision was made. It has taken the cat two years just to become comfortable with our family. Most people who visit us never see him because he still hides under the bed whenever anyone comes around.

Because we host a lot of outreach teams in our building, we must constantly remind those staying with us to keep our front and back door closed or Buddy, as we call him, will be so frightened by all the strangers that he might run away. Recently, while a team was staying with us, I noticed that Buddy had disappeared. I woke up early one morning and realized that he had not come out all night. I searched under every bed and in every corner. My heart began to race as I realized that Buddy was nowhere to be found. Without waking the children, I searched outside frantically. Never before had I experienced so much unrest. My mind was flooded with the thought of having to tell my children that we had lost this cat, who meant so much to my family. It seemed unbearable in light of all the loss we had already experienced. As I continued frantically retracing my steps, I begged the Lord for help. How could this happen? Why would God allow it? Surely He knew this would devastate my kids! I felt a panic that I had never experienced in my life. Moments later I found him. Someone had left the basement door open and he was hiding under shelving, crouched and shivering. I had to drag him out from under it. After taking him back inside our house, I went into the bathroom and wept. I cried not only out of thankfulness, but because I realized how frightened and immobilized I had become through the possibility of losing Buddy. I realized that I was truly afraid of the future. I wept like a small child after experiencing a terrible nightmare. I was overwhelmed at the reality of how vulnerable I felt. I simply heard the Lord gently ask me if I trusted Him.

When we experience tragic loss, the thought of experiencing loss in the future, even in lesser degrees, can be overwhelming and can steal our ability to rest in the Lord. I knew that the possibility of future loss was a reality that my kids and I would have to live with. How could we possibly walk in contentment after becoming intimately aware of how painful this world could be? I felt the Lord remind me that I could face my future with contentment because He loved me as His child and was committed to give me strength, grace, and redemption in all possible circumstances. We are not orphans. God will not abandon us. Christ reminded His disciples that He would not leave them as orphans (John 14:18). Furthermore, as Psalm 32:7 declares, God is our hiding place; He will protect us from trouble and surround us with songs of deliverance. Like Paul said, the secret was in knowing that I could do all things through Christ who strengthens me. His love, both protective and responsive, endures forever!

Our contentment is also directly related to what holds the greatest value in our lives, a value that cannot be stolen regardless of our circumstances. In 1 Timothy 6:6–7, Paul encourages Timothy that "Godliness with contentment is great gain. For we brought nothing into the world, and we can take nothing out of it." The focus of this scripture is to fix our gaze on what is truly valuable and, as Colossians 3:2 states, to "set [our] minds on things above, not on earthly things." Jesus declared in Luke 14:26, "If anyone comes to me and does not hate his father and mother, his wife and children, his brothers and sisters—yes, even his own life—he cannot be my disciple." Only when we have the Lord and His desires as our greatest priority will we be able to effectively follow Him. If there is anything else that we hold on to as a greater value, it can become the very thing that hinders us from a total obedience to the Lord.

Four months before Sherry and I were married, we were involved in a terrible van accident. Our ministry team was traveling home after completing a two-month outreach. Several of us were sleeping on the floor and bench seats of the van when it went into the median of a highway, causing it to roll a couple of times. My wife and I were thrown from the van at sixty-five miles an hour only a few feet from the edge of the highway. When I came to, my first thought was for the whereabouts of Sherry. I could not move and was unable to see where she was. A team member came over to me, telling me that Sherry looked pretty bad and he did not know how she was doing. I thanked the Lord that she was still alive, but I remember very clearly the Lord asking me if I would continue serving Him without her.

The founder of Youth With A Mission, Loren Cunningham, recounts a similar story of having to give his wife, Darlene, to the Lord after she had become lifeless in a car accident. Because of the lesson I had learned from Loren, I had already given Sherry to the Lord. But at that moment I realized what it would mean to go on without her. I told the Lord at that time, and many other times since, that no matter what happened, I would continue serving Him. It was a common practice of our family to quickly release to the Lord all of the good gifts that He had given us. After Sherry died, it was never a question of whether I would continue serving Him. That decision had already been made. This conclusion was brought about not because I had reached a superior level of spirituality but rather because I had become so aware of the Lord's worth and value that any other conclusion would be foolish. Because of the value of our Lord and because of His power in our lives, Christians of all people should be characterized by contentment. I am suggesting that true contentment is a result of our confidence in God's unending commitment toward us and the revelation of His incredible worth in the face of difficulty and hardship. This confidence yields the ability to experience a truly supernatural rest.

It is important to understand that biblical contentment is not another form of fatalism. Contentment in the Lord does not take away our action but creates the confidence for it. While we can be content for our own lives, I believe we are never really content with what we are able to give to the Lord's honor and glory. Biblical contentment was never meant to be a command of resignation that steals our desire to fight for our intended purpose. Is it possible to be content and dissatisfied at the same time? Can we be content about some things but dissatisfied about others and still be walking in godly contentment? The answer is an emphatic yes! Contentment that causes complacency and inaction is a misplaced contentment. The cry for redemption in our losses is not primarily for what it will bring to us, but what it will bring to the Lord. In our desire to show contentment in all things, we can become pacifistic in our jealous passion for that which belongs to God. We are called to fight for our fruitfulness because He is worthy of the original intent that He has placed on our lives. It is the Lord's glory and honor that our losses ultimately seek to steal. We must walk in contentment while maintaining a jealousy over that which belongs to the Lord. We will not walk in expectation of all that God desires to do in our lives, and therefore be unable to extend our faith and action toward those things, if we do not learn this paradox of Christian faith: contentment with dissatisfaction.

Often the way we portray the doctrine of biblical thankfulness and contentment steals our ability to respond to suffering and injustice. We run the risk of portraying to the world a God who does not take seriously the devastation we feel when our own hearts tell us that we were made for greater things. True scriptural thanksgiving and contentment is meant to remind us of God's fighting and enduring love on our behalf. It does not speak of His inactivity, but rather His jealous and faithful commitment toward our redemption. May our desperate and suffering world be introduced to the greatness of God through our ability to be truly thankful in all circumstances.

Father, as I feel the pain and loss of my broken world, I am reminded of who You are. You are the great and awesome God who has brought the world into existence through perfect love and wisdom. You have called me your child. I am not alone and helpless but am under Your great care. My heart is full of thankfulness for Your goodness and the position You have given me in Your heart. As I consider Your unfailing love, I am filled with expectation that You will defend my cause and secure my fruitfulness. You will come to my aid and restore my soul. I give You thanks for Your faithfulness that endures through all my pain.

PART II

BECOMING AGENTS
OF REDEMPTION
IN A BROKEN WORLD

Worthy is the Lamb, who was slain, to receive power
and wealth and wisdom and strength and
honor and glory and praise!

—REVELATION 5:12—

CHAPTER 7

GUARDING YOUR FRUITFULNESS

*"Then the man who had received the one talent came. 'Master,'
he said, 'I knew that you are a hard man, harvesting where
you have not sown and gathering where you have not scattered seed. So I was afraid and went out and hid your
talent in the ground. See, here is what belongs to you.'"*

—Matthew 25:24–25—

O
UR CONFIDENCE IN God's redeeming nature not only brings
an expectation and hope for living, but it also creates a
boldness to step out in the unique calling and destiny that
the Lord has placed on our lives. That destiny is to colabor with Him
in seeing that which belongs to Him redeemed. Part of our redemption is seeing the return of that God-intended glory on our lives. As
we discussed in Isaiah 61, it is those who have exchanged the ashes of
their lives for the beauty the Lord provides that are destined to become
a "display of his splendor" (v. 3). Our personal redemption is not truly
complete until we walk once again in the God-given ability to display
His image as a Redeemer to others. Through the transforming work of
Christ, we are given the honor of not only partaking of His redeeming
nature but also fellowshiping with His redemptive purposes in the
world. Yet, in spite of this glorious destiny, our past hurt can cause a
hesitation towards future risk. The situations dealt to us by this broken

and fallen world can challenge our confidence in finishing the race marked out for us by God.

Every year at our Youth With A Mission center in Chicago, we host a five-month training school called the School of Urban Frontiers. This had been my and my wife's vision for a few years, and we held our first school in the fall of 2002. Sherry had carried much of the vision to mobilize this generation into the frontiers of our urban centers. We were preparing to host our second school when she was diagnosed with cancer. In fact, the school started just three weeks after she died. I was scheduled to speak that first week of the school. After Sherry died, we all prayed as a staff and felt that we were to go ahead with the school as planned.

I woke up the morning of that first week petrified with the thought of walking into that classroom. All of a sudden, I did not feel that I could bring vision and faith to these students. I felt empty. I struggled with the Lord—that He should ask me to do this. I told the Lord I just simply did not have what was needed to fulfill this responsibility. How could He expect this of me? I felt the Lord tell me to trust Him and went through with it anyway. Surprisingly, I sensed His heart as I taught and found the vision that had once been there before. Over the next few months from that first week of the school, I faced several other similar situations. That same sense of barrenness was there as I would prepare to lead the team on some evangelistic ministry project. It would be there as I was expected to pray over someone else's need with faith. Sometimes it was as simple as giving thanks before a meal or praying with my children before they went to bed.

I remember one evening feeling very angry. It was one thing that I should have to face the pain of losing Sherry, but to go on in ministry without the confidence that I once had just seemed too much. I felt truly handicapped. It was during this time that the Lord showed me a passage out of Matthew 25. Jesus had been saying many things to

His disciples in response to a question raised in Matthew 24:3. His disciples asked Him, "What will be the sign of your coming and of the end of the age?" Then in Matthew 25:1 Jesus says, "At that time the kingdom of heaven will be like…" followed by three parables about the activities of the kingdom of heaven in the last days. It's here that we read what has commonly been called the parable of the talents. I used to cringe when I read this parable because I could not help feeling that the judgment passed on the third servant was kind of harsh. After all, it's not like he squandered his master's possessions. He just did nothing with the talent, and in return he is cast out into the darkness where there was "weeping and gnashing of teeth" (v. 30). I would like to suggest that there is much to this parable that relates to this generation. To get a full glimpse of what is taking place let's consider the details of the story.

Because this story is a parable, we can assume that the aspects of the story represent something else. We also know that this relates to how God's kingdom will operate in the last days. The story starts with a master calling his servants to him and entrusting his property to them. He then gives them each different amounts of his possessions to take care of.

> To one he gave five talents of money, to another two talents, and to another one talent, each according to his ability. Then he went on his journey. The man who had received the five talents went at once and put his money to work and gained five more. So also, the one with the two talents gained two more. But the one who had received the one talent went off, dug a hole in the ground and hid his master's money. After a long time the master of the servants returned and settled accounts with them.
>
> —Matthew 25:15–19

Because this is a parable of the End Times, I believe it is about the activity of the church in multiplying the prized possessions of our Lord until He returns. Notice that the master goes on a journey and then returns after "a long time" to settle accounts. This story is about us, and we are waiting for the return of our Lord Jesus. When He returns, He will want to know what we have done with His treasures. I would also like to suggest that the treasures of our Lord could only be the nations, for which He has paid a great price for their redemption. Speaking of the Lamb of God, Revelation 5:9 says, "You are worthy to take the scroll and to open its seals, because you were slain, and with your blood you purchased men for God from every tribe and language and people and nation." Surely this song in heaven is a fulfillment of the promise given in Psalm 2. Commonly considered a messianic psalm (speaking of the Messiah), verses 7 and 8 say, "I will proclaim the decree of the LORD: He said to me, 'You are my Son; today I have become your Father. Ask of me, and I will make the nations your inheritance, the ends of the earth your possession.'" Truly, there can be no other possession of consequence to the Lord.

The Lord has entrusted the care and evangelization of the nations to His church. The fact that He gave His possessions in different measure, I believe, relates to the different responsibilities that He has given to each generation in order to be fruitful in multiplying His prized possessions. The story is about how each generation has handled being entrusted with such an honor. You know the story. The servant with five came back with five more, and the one with two came back with two more. Then there was the third servant who buried the master's treasure, giving it back to him when he returned. Why was the master so upset about the way the third servant handled things? Let's look at two components of this story that are very important.

AN ISSUE OF ABILITY

First, in verse 15 it says that the master gave to "each according to his ability." Interestingly, this is the only time in the New Testament where this Greek word is translated "ability." It is translated over seventy other times as "power." It's used in reference to God's power or a supernatural power from God. The word in Greek is *dunamis*. It actually means "miraculous power," according to Strong's Greek dictionary. It is usually, by implication, a miracle itself. In other words, the Lord has entrusted His possessions to us not according to our own ability but His. He has empowered us with miraculous power to accomplish this task. The third servant said he hid the talent because he knew that the master was "a hard man, harvesting where he had not sown and gathering where he had not scattered seed" (v. 24). This was a false accusation. By saying it, he not only misrepresents the truth but also shows that he does not know his master. As we will see in another chapter, I believe that this accusation comes directly from Satan. It is this spirit that the Lord judges so harshly. It is the kind of spirit that robs us of our confidence in times of loss and weariness.

Often, when we are experiencing the reoccurring pains of some tragedy, disappointment, or wrong, we wonder how we can possibly continue fulfilling God's purposes in our lives. We may be emotionally empty and tired. Perhaps the very things or people that once gave us confidence are no longer there. I had prepared myself for the emotional loss of my wife and best friend. It hurts deeply to lose something of such value. But I was not prepared for the havoc brought to my ability to continue with confidence in the call of God on my life. The spiritual fervor and sharpness that my relationship with Sherry had provided was now profoundly missing. I could not see my world through the same spiritual lenses. It's at these moments that we can begin to listen to the lies of the enemy: "It's just not fair that God should require you to do this; it's not realistic. God is so cruel. He just expects you to look inside yourself and find some strength that He knows is not there. It's just like God to demand fruitfulness from your life without giving you what you need to do it."

We must reject these accusations and remember who the Lord is. In the wake of loss, it is not enough to just ignore our feelings of inadequacy. We must address these realities with the truth of His commitment toward us. He has actually provided everything we need to be fruitful and to fulfill His calling on our lives. He has given to each of us His own miraculous power. It is not His character to demand where He has not sown. In verse 25 the servant says, "So I was afraid and went out and hid your talent." The result of listening to these accusations against God is a fear that robs our ability to take risk, to be vulnerable, and to expect God to move in our lives. We can do God an injustice by not expecting Him to provide what we need, even in our most desolate times. He has promised to give us what we need as we walk in obedience to His call on our lives.

AN ISSUE OF INTIMACY

The second important thing to notice about the third servant's response was what he said to the master in returning the talent given to him. In verse 25 he says, "See, here is what belongs to you." In other words, he never took ownership in what was entrusted to him. He did not care for that which concerned his master. In verses 21 and 23 we can see the contrast with the other two servants when the reward for their fruitfulness was mentioned: "Well done, good and faithful servant! You have been faithful with a few things; I will put you in charge of many things. Come and share your master's happiness." The reward was not only the chance to share in more of that which concerned the master, but to share in his very happiness. It was an offer to be intimate with the Lord's prized possessions. This is our glory and honor! The unfaithful servant had no regard for this honor. His disregard was an indication that he did not see or know the value of partnering with the Lord in His dreams for the world.

The enemy of our souls seeks to steal our fruitfulness and ultimately the honor that he himself lost—to be intimate with the Lord's heart. This generation is threatened by a fear that is unfounded. Our loss and the awareness of extreme loss in others has challenged our perspective of who God is. God has not only given us the honor and glory of carrying His concerns, but He has given us a miraculous power to finish what He has called us to do. Paul uses this same Greek word for miraculous power in Ephesians 1:18–21. Consider how great this power is that God has made available to you.

> I pray also that the eyes of your heart may be enlightened in order that you may know the hope to which he has called you, the riches of his glorious inheritance in the saints, and his incomparably great power [*dunamis*] for us who believe. That power is like the working of his mighty strength, which he exerted in Christ when he raised him from the dead and seated him at his right hand in heavenly realms, far above all rule and authority, power and dominion, and every title that can be given, not only in the present age but also in the one to come.

Every single morning since Sherry died, I am hit with the overwhelming emotions of lack and emptiness the moment I open my eyes. It's at that moment that the fruitfulness of my day is challenged. When we remind ourselves of the incredible passion the Lord has for our fruitfulness, we are able to take back that "hope to which He has called [us]."

A BARREN FIG TREE

In Matthew 21, we are given a fascinating glimpse into that deep longing the Lord has for our fruitfulness. It follows the climactic record of Jesus entering for the first time the city of Jerusalem. Consider the history that led to this moment. For four thousand years God has invested in the children of Israel. He gave them the privilege of being a nation chosen to reveal His character and grace to all the nations of the world. In 2 Chronicles 6:6 God says, "I have chosen Jerusalem for my Name to be there." Imagine the anticipation of our Lord when entering the very city over which, for thousands of years, He had spoken so many words of promise. I find that these first activities of our Lord upon entering this city are of great importance. One of the first things that take place is outlined in a curious passage in Matthew 21:18–22:

> Early in the morning, as he was on his way back to the city, he was hungry. Seeing a fig tree by the road, he went up to it but found nothing on it except leaves. Then he said to it, "May you never bear fruit again!" Immediately the tree withered. When the disciples saw this, they were amazed. "How did the fig tree wither so quickly?" they asked. Jesus replied, "I tell you the truth, if you have faith and do not doubt, not only can you do what was done to the fig tree, but also you can say to this mountain, 'Go, throw yourself into the sea,' and it will be done. If you believe, you will receive whatever you ask for in prayer."

This, by the way, is the only recorded miracle of Jesus where something is cursed rather than brought to life or growth. It seems that Jesus was deeply frustrated. What is curious about this situation is revealed to us in a parallel passage found in Mark 11:12–14. In verse 13, Mark adds that when Jesus reached the tree, "He found nothing but leaves, because it was not the season for figs." Surely Jesus must have known that the tree would not have had figs because it was not the season. In other words, this whole situation must have had very little to do with the fig tree itself, but rather something it represented upon entering Jerusalem for the very first time. Equally curious is the way in which Jesus answers His disciples' amazement at the encounter. He does not explain why He cursed the tree. Rather, He turns to them with a great challenge of faith and promise. Have you ever witnessed an unusual action of someone near you, and when asked what he or she was doing, they unload on you an intense communication that seems to have nothing to do with your question? Often it is because at that moment they are actually revealing the very consuming thoughts that must have led up to the unusual action. I would like to suggest that this is what we are witnessing in this passage.

Compare this account with Isaiah 5:1–7. God is communicating His frustration over the children of Israel. Verses 1–4 say:

> I will sing for the one I love a song about his vineyard: My loved one had a vineyard on a fertile hillside. He dug it up and cleared it of stones and planted it with the choicest vines. He built a watchtower in it and cut out a winepress as well. Then he looked for a crop of good grapes, but it yielded only bad fruit. Now you dwellers in Jerusalem and men of Judah, judge between me and my vineyard. What more could have been done for my vineyard than I have done for it? When I looked for good grapes, why did it yield only bad?

Verses 5 and 6 continue with the Lord proclaiming His removal of blessing and the following devastation of His vineyard. Verse 7 gives us an understanding into what the vineyard represented.

> The vineyard of the LORD Almighty is the house of Israel, and the men of Judah are the garden of his delight. And he looked for justice, but saw bloodshed; for righteousness, but heard cries of distress.

I believe that what we are witnessing in Matthew 21 is the fulfill-ment of this scripture. The Lord enters His city and expects fruit from all that He has invested in the children of Israel but instead finds nothing. Jesus' response to His disciples is the same as that of the Father in Isaiah 5. He is saying, "What more could I have done for my vineyard? I have invested all that is needed for its fruitfulness. I have removed all obstacles, and I have even placed a watch over it day and night so that no enemy may steal from it. My anticipation has been greatly disappointed. But, truly I tell you now, if you will only believe, rely, and trust in what I have given you, responding in instant obedi-ence to what I tell you to do, you could even say to this mountain, 'Be thrown into the sea,' and it would be done."

God's confidence in our ability to do His will is far greater than ours. It's because He knows what He has invested in us. Our ability to follow through in what the Lord has entrusted to us, even in the midst of great loss or pain, has nothing to do with our strengths, but everything to do with His. The enemy seeks to steal our expectation of fruitfulness by getting us to focus on what we have to offer rather than what the Lord is willing to offer through us. God has placed a guard over our fruitfulness. We must do the same. We must be a generation that is jealous over what the Lord has invested in us. Let us not so quickly concede our honor and His glory in our weakness. I would like to suggest that we not only have reason to expect God to work in us, but it is the glory due His name that we should expect Him to work His power in us, regardless of our weakness.

The Bible talks about Jesus taking the sting of death away because we have a confidence that to be separate from the body is to be present with the Lord, which is far better. (See 2 Corinthians 5:8, KJV; 1 Corin-thians 15:55–56.) I am discovering that there is a sting to living as well. The sting comes when we are forced to live in the midst of great loss. One of the effects of this stinging existence is the constant reminder of our inability to bring forth anything of lasting beauty for the One who deserves far more than we could ever give Him. We were made for fruitfulness.

The very value of our existence is found in the opportunity we have, as those made in God's image, to bring forth some unique testimony of His greatness that may be seen for all of eternity. Loss can make us feel as though our hands are suddenly tied. To be forced to continue living without the ability to fulfill the reason for our existence is worse than death. Yet our fruitfulness is not dependent on our own abilities or affected by the brokenness of our lives. Regardless of what we have experienced, our fruitfulness has always been the result of the Lord's commitment to reap only where He has sown. Truly He has sown much in each of us that cannot be taken away—except by our own refusal to acknowledge its existence.

When the pains of your past cause you to hesitate in carrying the intimate heart of the Father for His world, remember that He has not left you alone in your calling. He is not a God who would demand from us without being willing to provide for our success. He has great faith in Himself to accomplish great things in you. We will look in the next few chapters at some of the unique ways that we can display God's splendor, in spite of our broken lives. If we are not convinced of God's provision to fulfill that destiny, we will be robbed of the opportunity to "share in the master's happiness."

Lord, there are times when I feel like I do not have what is needed to give You what You ask. But I know that You have invested Your power in my fruitfulness. I will not listen to the enemy's lies about You. I so long to give You what You deserve. Reveal Your power in me, Lord. I will trust in You. Give me a heart of unhesitating obedience. May You receive that which belongs to You, for Your Name's sake.

CHAPTER 8

DEFENDING GOD'S NAME

"Does Job fear God for nothing?" Satan replied. "Have you not put a hedge around him and his household and everything he has? You have blessed the work of his hands, so that his flocks and herds are spread throughout the land. But stretch out your hand and strike everything he has, and he will surely curse you to your face.

—JOB 1:9–11—

S WE SEEK the Lord in understanding tragic loss, we are often encouraged to gain some comfort or revelation through the biblical testimony of the life of Job. The Book of Job is believed to be one of the oldest books in the Bible, and perhaps one of the most fascinating. Many theological books have been written about the themes presented in Job. I have been particularly interested in the very conversation between God and Satan. Usually the first chapter of a book gives us a foundation or even an explanation for the rest of the story. We would do well to consider what is actually taking place in this conversation. I have said previously in this book that perhaps the mistake of Job as he sought to understand God's justice in his suffering was that he was looking at his circumstances as if he and the Lord were the only ones involved. When God finally speaks in response to Job, He does not tell Job that he just can't understand what

God is like. Rather, he talks about the complexity of His creation and how He is governing its intended purpose. (See Job 38–41.)

Again, I would like to suggest that God does not need to create suffering in our lives to fulfill His purposes. Much of our suffering has been created and sustained by the will of His fallen creation. In response, God does not abandon His original plan for His world but is managing its redemption, while putting a limit of time on its suffering. In that first year after Sherry died, my seven-year-old son repeatedly communicated his wish that we could all just leave this earth now and go be with Mommy in heaven. My response has always been that I share that wish as well. But we then talk about how we must do our part to fulfill God's desires before we go. Then, I tell him, we will have something to give God when we arrive. It is important that we move from a focus of survival in our fallen world to understanding what God can bring forth through our lives that can last for eternity.

Often I am confronted in evangelism with the question: "If Satan is causing so many problems why doesn't God just judge him now and get rid of him?" I would like to suggest that the answer lies in *how* God is judging Satan. In understanding this, we not only get a glimpse of how God is governing His world, but we can perceive part of the Lord's intended glory for those He created in his image. After all, when Satan rebelled against the Lord, he was cast down to Earth. Adam and Eve, another part of God's creation, were expected to deal with him. If this action by God is considered strictly from an administrative point of view, then it would be easy to assume some lack of wisdom or mismanagement on God's part. As believers, we know this could not be true because the Scripture tells us that God created the world in perfect wisdom. (See Proverbs 8.) I believe this action reveals both the intimate calling placed on man by his Maker and the righteous ways of a just Judge in relation to one of His subjects.

I am going to suggest that the story of Job may have more to do with putting the devil on trial than putting Job on trial. This only makes sense if we believe that the Lord has given us, as those created in His image, some unique ability to play a part in the process of judging the accusations of God's enemies. Job's experience is, in my opinion, an extreme example of judging the enemy and an exception to the rule. Yet the aspect of how God is judging His enemies is a long story and one in which we can willingly play a part by the way we respond to loss. One way of looking at the tragic loss in Job's story is through how it might fulfill God's purpose strictly in Job's life. Yet, the entire conversation between God and Satan began by the Lord challenging the enemy in showing off Job's righteousness. The Lord was judging the rightness of Satan's rebellion by revealing another created being who did not find it difficult to walk uprightly before the Lord. It was when the enemy challenged that comparison between himself and Job that the story took a turn.

I do not believe the Lord was looking for an occasion to inflict suffering on Job, as if the Lord were seeking to test Job for his own satisfaction. In Job 2:3 God actually tells Satan, "You incited me against him to ruin him without any reason." It must have been a very difficult decision at that moment for the Lord. In some ways God was inviting Job, in a very intimate and vulnerable way, to play an extreme part in judging the enemy. God could have refused the challenge. Perhaps the Lord was able to make that decision both because of a trust He had in Job and a confidence in Himself to bring about redemption. I would like to suggest that, though Job's situation was extreme, all believers carry in some way a similar invitation to judge the accusations of God's enemies. By considering this aspect of our struggle in the fallen and broken world in which we live, we can gain a perspective of one of the unique and honorable callings placed on the brief story of our earthly existence. Let's look at a few passages that shed some light on this subject.

THE TESTIMONY OF JESUS

According to Scripture, the first Adam brought sin into the world but the second Adam (Jesus) has brought life and redemption to all things. The life and death of Jesus accomplished much for the redemption of God's original plan for creation. When God put on flesh and walked among us, He also provided a clear standard of reality. In John 16:8–11, Jesus told His disciples that He must go to the Father but He would send the Holy Spirit to remind them of the truth that He displayed on Earth.

> When he comes, he will convict the world of guilt in regard to sin and righteousness and judgment: in regard to sin, because men do not believe in me; in regard to righteousness, because I am going to the Father, where you can see me no longer; and in regard to judgment, because the prince of this world now stands condemned.

Men would no longer have the chance to see Jesus in the flesh, so the Holy Spirit would convict the world of the truth that Jesus' life displayed. The three things the Holy Spirit would convict men of are all equally important, but I want to focus on the last one. The scripture says that the Holy Spirit will convict men of judgment because the prince of this world now stands condemned. There are two different Greek words used for "judgment" and "condemnation" in this scripture. The word used for "judgment" is *krisis*, which means by implication, "justice being served." The word for "condemned" is *krimo*, which means "to have decided against, to call into question, to distinguish, conclude, accusation." In other words, the scripture could be understood as, "The Holy Spirit will convict men of true justice, because the prince of this world has been called into question, distinguished for who he is, and has been decided against." When Jesus put on humanity and yet walked in obedience even unto death, He brought judgment on the enemy. His life called into question the enemy's claims against God.

The enemy stood in the presence of God and yet accused Him of His lack of worthiness and right to rule. God had every right to condemn Satan in his rebellion, but as a righteous judge, I believe that God's desire is always to reveal what is true. God is light. It is His nature to reveal what is right, not just demand it. The enemy's claims against God have been the same since the beginning. Perhaps you have heard the enemy's accusations. He says that God is self-seeking and does not give us what we need to succeed. We saw that in Matthew 25. He also claims that those who disobey God find greater fulfillment because God is only trying to withhold good things. This was the very argument brought to Adam and Eve in Genesis 3. In addition, he claims that God has abandoned us and does not really care for our problems. In other words, the enemy says that God is not just, He is not good, and He is not faithful. Interestingly, these are the three arguments used by an unbelieving world to justify their independence from God.

The life of Jesus confronted each of these accusations, showing them for the fallacies that they were. Though we did not deserve it, God went out of His way to provide the power we need to succeed in His original plan for our lives. The life of Jesus showed that our Father is an extravagant giver. He gave His greatest so we could experience true life. The sacrifice of Jesus on the cross shows that He does not abandon us in our failure. God confronted these accusations in the beginning when He promised redemption to Adam and Eve. Every generation from that time was given the opportunity to believe on that promise, and when Jesus came He brought it to the light once and for all. The enemy's claims for all of eternity will be found wanting by the presence of our Lord and the scars on His hands and feet.

THE TESTIMONY OF GOD'S CHILDREN

Not only does the blood of Jesus bring into question the enemy's claims against God, but our lives do as well. In 1 Corinthians 6:3, Paul mentions a peculiar verse in response to a crisis in the Corinthian church. He was rebuking them for taking their cases of justice before the worldly courts instead of dealing with it themselves. In 1 Corinthians 6:2–3, it states:

> Do you not know that the saints will judge the world? And if you are to judge the world, are you not competent to judge trivial cases? Do you not know that we will judge angels? How much more the things of this life!

The Greek word for *judge* in this verse is the same as the word *condemnation* in John 16. It is "to call into question, distinguish between, and conclude what is true and what is false."

I used to feel uncomfortable about this verse. It just seemed weird that I would have to sit in some judge's chair, so to speak, and pass sentencing on the fallen angels as they paraded by my court. I know now that this is not what is meant by this scripture. It is God who will pass sentencing on all of His creation. It's not what we will do in heaven that will judge the angels but our lives lived here on Earth. As a created being, the enemy seeks to justify his rebellion through you. This is what we see in Job 1:6–11. When Satan came before God, the Lord brought Job to his attention. It was as much to say, "Do you see Job? He fears me and knows the truth." Satan's response was a challenge: "Just remove your blessing and He will see you for the God that you truly are." Perhaps God was not so much allowing the enemy to justify his claims about Job, but rather God was allowing Job the honor of defending what was true and thereby judging the enemy. This only makes sense in the context of our calling, as those created in His image, to exist in intimate friendship with our Maker. It would be an honor to defend the name of our loving Father.

As frail humans, we have a unique opportunity to distinguish, call into question, and decide against the enemy's claims about God. Satan stood in the very presence of God, beholding His glory, and yet accused His character. We see God through a veil, enduring great suffering and yet witnessing of God's character and trustworthiness. I believe this is our honor. Though it is not the focus of our desire to simply judge the enemy, defending the name of our God is an honor that we should not lightly esteem.

The Scripture speaks of a generation that seeks the very face of God. As we looked at earlier, Psalms 24 says the people of this generation will be characterized as he who "has clean hands and a pure heart, who does not lift up his soul to an idol or swear by what is false" (v. 4). It goes on to say that "he will receive blessing from the LORD and vindication from God his savior. Such is the generation of those who seek him, who seek your face, O God of Jacob" (vv. 5–6). The generation spoken of in this passage will be recognized by its desire for purity and its unwavering commitment to what is true. That commitment is tested and revealed most in the midst of great suffering and loss. The nature of a world in which God is accused by His enemies of being unjust creates an opportunity for each generation to rise to the expectation and honor of defending His name and silencing His enemies. How will we defend God's name in the midst of suffering? Will we swear by what is false or what is true? Will we listen to the false accusations of God's enemies, or will we stand by His character? When the enemy claims that God is not just, how will we defend the rightness of His actions? When the goodness of God is challenged, how will we respond? When our broken world accuses God of a lack of faithfulness, how will we help people see His commitment to our redemption?

Listen to the words of the prophet Habakkuk in Habakkuk 3:17–18:

> Though the fig tree does not bud and there are no grapes on the vines, though the olive crop fails and the fields produce no food, though there are no sheep in the pen and no cattle in the stalls, yet I will rejoice in the LORD, I will be joyful in God my Savior.

This was not simply a dutiful response to a difficult situation. It was founded on an understanding of who he knew his God to be. Verse 19 says "The Sovereign LORD is my strength; he makes my feet like the feet of a deer, he enables me to go on the heights." The focus is on who God is and what He will do for us.

Honoring His Name

In Malachi 3:13–18 we read an interesting account of God's frustration over wrongful accusations against Him by His people, and we get a glimpse of His desire for a people who honor His name.

> "You have said harsh things against me," says the LORD. "Yet you ask, 'What have we said against you?' You have said, 'It is futile to serve God. What did we gain by carrying out his requirements and going about like mourners before the LORD Almighty? But now we call the arrogant blessed. Certainly the evildoers prosper, and even those who challenge God escape.'" Then those who feared the LORD talked with each other, and the LORD listened and heard. A scroll of remembrance was written in his presence concerning those who feared the LORD and honored his name. "They will be mine," says the LORD Almighty, "in the day when I make up my treasured possession. I will spare them, just as in compassion a man spares his

son who serves him. And you will again see the distinction between the righteous and the wicked, between those who serve God and those who do not."

The ear of God is tuned in to the way in which we defend His name. His treasured possession will be made up of those who honor Him. The people who are committed to His honor are the ones in which He can entrust the deepest secrets of His heart. I believe this generation is poised to be just such a people. In the face of a broken and painful existence, we can declare His name and judge the wrongful claims of this world and God's enemies. Satan continues to accuse the church before God. He wants to prove that his rebellion was justified. God has chosen to honor us with the opportunity to play a part in this judgment. Take a look at Revelation 12:10–11:

> Then I heard a loud voice in heaven say, "Now have come the salvation and the power and the kingdom of our God, and the authority of his Christ. For the accuser of our brothers, who accuses them before our God day and night, has been hurled down. They overcame him by the blood of the Lamb and by the word of their testimony; they did not love their lives so much as to shrink from death."

Notice that the church overcame the enemy first by the testimony of the work of Christ and then by their own testimony. Our testimony is the unique story of God's loving commitment and redemption in our lives. It's the way in which God reveals His greatness through our broken and fallen lives. The opportunity to defend God's name and rightly represent His beauty is a point of intimacy in our relationship with the Lord and an expression of our intended glory. I find it hard to believe that those spoken of in this passage, who loved not their lives so much as to shrink from death, feel that it was unfair that they suffered so much. Rather, they have been honored before their

God. For all of eternity they can celebrate that they had the opportunity, through that short and fleeting existence on Earth, to love and worship with their very lives the most worthy being in the universe. God's treasured possession will not be made of those who simply did grand things for God, but of those who loved God in a grand way. It is the glory of God to love His creation and the glory of the creation to love its God.

After my wife died, I felt both great grief and a desire to see God have the opportunity to reveal His greatness through the pain my family felt. That greatness is revealed not in making sense out of Sherry's death but in giving my family a story of His justice, goodness, and faithfulness in response to her death. Someday, God will restore all things, but this short life is my family's only chance to show God what He means to us. While I share the desire of my son to leave this earth as quickly as possible and go to my true home, I would not want to lose my opportunity here on Earth to give God that which He deserves.

Make that choice to love God in a grand way. I am not suggesting that you ignore the pain and injustice that you have faced. God surely doesn't ignore it. But claim your right to defend God's name in response to your brokenness. Be a part of that generation that seeks the very face of God. The world is hungry to see this God who is committed to them and has not left them alone. It is the story of your life that will show it to them. Rather than defending Himself, God often waits for His children to rise to that honor.

In Numbers 25, we read the account of how Moab had seduced Israel to dishonor their God. The Moabites feared the Israelites would destroy them, so they conspired to send their women into the camp of the Israelites to seduce them, causing them to worship and sacrifice to Baal. Without shame the Israelites committed adultery with the Moabite women and worshiped their god. God was roused to anger, and Moses called the leaders together. During this time an Israelite man shamelessly brought his Moabite mistress to his family's tent in front of everyone. Then Phinehas, the grandson of Aaron, grabs a spear and, following the man into his tent, stabs both the man and woman at the same time. God then declares in verses 10–11:

> Phinehas son of Eleazer, the son of Aaron, the priest, has turned my anger away from the Israelites; for he was as zealous as I am for my honor among them, so that in my zeal I did not put an end to them.

God was so blessed by Phinehas's response that He goes on to make a covenant with him and his descendants, that they would have the honor of serving as priests continuously, "because he was zealous for the honor of his God" (v. 13). I am not advocating that we go about throwing spears. The life of Jesus revealed a much more powerful way of defending God—by living a life of obedience no matter the cost. God will wait for us to defend His honor. We do that by jealously giving the Lord His right to redeem us through our loss and show the emptiness of the enemy's claims against God

I imagine that when we all get to heaven we will be surprised about many things. For sure the beauty and greatness of our God will be more than we could have anticipated. Scripture also tells us that we will all be surprised at the smallness of the accuser who conquered kingdoms and led countless astray by his lies. (See Isaiah 14:12–17.) I tend to believe that we will be surprised by the glory that has been placed on our existence as well. In an effort to maintain a sense of humility in our lives, we tend to downplay our significance and beauty. I would like to suggest that in doing so we are actually lessening God's glory. When you admire the beauty and majesty of a great work of art, it is the artist you are praising, not the art itself—the art reflects the artist. The art had no power to bring itself into existence; it was created by the wise and talented hands of the craftsman. When we look back on our lives lived here on Earth, we will be amazed at the power, authority, and beauty that the Lord placed on us, individually and corporately. Not only does the enemy lie to us about God, but he lies to us about ourselves. They are both attacks against the Lord's greatness. Perhaps in our modern culture we have lost the sense of nobility, honor, and sacrificing for a great cause. We have been burned by causes thought to be good, only to be seen as something other than good in the end. We are even teaching our children to look at history with skepticism. Our heroes display immorality and our leaders show self-interest. Our children no longer dream of championing great causes because we simply don't believe any cause can be truly good. We spend our lives with no greater aspiration than to live as comfortably as we can and hopefully die at an old age. In other times, men would have rather died than live that way. We are being robbed of our significance and don't even know it.

When God created us in His image, we were meant for greatness—not a greatness that we could produce apart from God but one given to us by God. Though "we do not wrestle against flesh and blood" (Eph. 6:12, NKJV), we are called to take captive every thought "that exalts itself against the knowledge of God" (2 Cor.10:5, NKJV), champion God's causes, and fill His creation with righteousness and truth. This earth is not our home. We are here to write a story that will be read to God's glory for all of eternity. Scripture commands us to do everything in the name of Jesus. This is more than remembering to add a phrase at the end of our prayers. It is a challenge to live for a cause—the cause of Christ—to defend His name and honor, and to show to a dying and broken world the victories that Christ has won for them.

The scars and suffering of your life offer you a unique opportunity to shine in your intended glory. It's your right and your honor. Don't let anyone steal it from you. It's time for you to shine!

Lord, I am attracted to You. Your character is trustworthy. All the enemy's claims against You are false. Write Your glory on the story of my life. I desire to see Your face. Thank You for honoring my existence, by giving me both the opportunity and ability to love You. It does not matter what this fallen world does to me; it will never change who You are. You are the one who strengthens me and stoops down to make me great. You deserve the right to take center stage in my life. Raise up a generation, Lord, that is committed to purity and does not swear by what is false. You deserve the right to be seen for who You truly are. May Your goodness shine through our lives.

CHAPTER 9

REDEEMING HONOR

You have kept your promise because you are righteous.

—Nehemiah 9:8—

*Honor your father and mother, as the LORD your God has
commanded you, so that you may live long and that it may go
well with you in the land the LORD your God is giving you.*

—Deuteronomy 5:16—

G OD IS COMMITTED to redemption and restoration, not only
in our lives but also over His purposes in history. The
pursuit of these things in our world must be a partnership
with the Lord. It is the challenge of our generation to embrace the
redemption God has planned for our broken world as well as answer
the cries of hopelessness around us. Often the redemption of our individual destiny is linked to the redemption of those to whom the Lord
has connected us. How do we partner with God's desire to redeem
what He has envisioned and initiated throughout history? I have
discovered that not everything I put my hands to has experienced the
Lord's blessing. His will is always consistent with His character. Therefore, when we know God's ways, we are able to develop ministry and
lifestyles that are in accordance with how He has intended to display
His story of faithfulness. God is a God who honors. He honors His

promises and His name; He honors faith and obedience; He desires to honor us! The generation that will see great fruitfulness for God's kingdom will be the one that can partner with the Lord's desire to both honor His promises throughout history and redeem the honor of those who have gone before us.

A COVENANT-KEEPING GOD

The Ten Commandments of the Lord, described in Deuteronomy 5:6–21, were not invented by God to simply help us manage society, but they are in fact a description of what God is like. We are commanded to have no other gods but the one true God, because He is a God who is always committed to that which is true. We are commanded to not kill, steal, or lie, because He would never do these things. The Ten Commandments give us a glimpse of the character of our God and therefore describe our intended purpose as those created in His image. One of the aspects of God's character that greatly affects our destiny is the commitment He has toward fulfilling His covenants throughout history. This aspect of His nature is represented in the command to honor our father and mother.

It is interesting that the commandment to honor our father and mother is the only commandment with a promise attached to it. If we obey this command, the Lord promises that we will experience long life and that it will go well with the land the Lord has given us. Remember that the allotment of land to the Israelites is what gave them a significant role in displaying God's faithfulness in the world. Our land may be the visions, dreams, and callings that God has given us. In other words, this commandment comes with a promise to finish the race marked out for us and experience fruitfulness in what the Lord has invested in our lives. We long to see the visions and callings of the Lord on our lives fulfilled. Perhaps this command gives us a key to releasing God's blessing on our fruitfulness.

What does this commandment say about the character of our God? Why is it so important to honor our parents that we are promised our own fruitfulness to the degree that we fulfill this command? The honoring mentioned in this passage is not confined to simply giving respect or doing what we are told by our elders but rather is a command to recognize God's investment in the generations that have gone before us. The Hebrew word translated here for *honor* comes from the expression of giving something weight. It means "to recognize the importance of something, to give it unique and special significance." God wants us to recognize the importance of those who have gone before us and how His purposes in their lives affect His destiny on ours. God is a covenant-keeping God. It is His nature and the name by which He has chosen to be remembered. (See Exodus 3:14–15.) He is jealously committed to fulfilling those covenants. He is a God who enters into relationship with those who fear Him, righteously fulfilling any promise He has made to those relationships. Often the fulfillment of these covenants is actualized through future generations. That covenant line is broken when we are unable to give "weight" to those who have gone before us.

We are tempted, through our culture of individualism, to see God as a young God. Though we would never claim this theology, we sometimes act as though God has only existed since our birth in this world. We do this by evaluating our world and its significance simply by those things that have occurred in our lifetime. The generation that will truly see God's redemptive plans come into existence is the one that can see God's investments throughout history and be willing to see themselves as a possible return on those investments. I believe it is the glory of the young to crown the old and the power of the old to validate the young. By this I mean that it is an expression of our intended glory to allow God to fulfill through us His covenants in previous generations, and it is the promises of God, given to previous generations, that are meant to validate the importance of our actions.

Every generation longs to be recognized for their importance. We want the older generation to not only bless us but also validate the emerging role that we play in history. It is the desire of the older generation to have their sacrifices and investments in this world recognized by the young, hoping that the promised returns of their labor will not be lost. None of this will be realized unless we are connected to history and respect the role it plays in our destinies. Our fruitfulness is dependent on our commitment to honor God's activity and intended purposes throughout history.

PARTNERING WITH THE PAST

We see a great example of this kind of honoring through the life of Solomon in relation to his father, David. In 1 Kings Solomon prays to the Lord concerning the temple he had built for the Lord's name. He prays:

> "My father David had it in his heart to build a temple for the Name of the LORD, the God of Israel. But the LORD said to my father David, 'Because it was in your heart to build a temple for my Name, you did well to have this in your heart. Nevertheless, you are not the one to build the temple, but your son, who is your own flesh and blood—he is the one who will build the temple for my Name.' The LORD has kept the promise he made: I have succeeded David my father and now I sit on the throne of Israel, just as the LORD promised, and I have built the temple for the Name of the LORD, the God of Israel."
>
> —1 Kings 8:17–20

> "O LORD, God of Israel, there is no God like you in heaven above or on the earth below—you who keep your covenant of love with your servants who continue wholeheartedly in your

way. You have kept your promise to your servant David my father; with your mouth you have promised and with your hand you have fulfilled it—as it is today. Now LORD, God of Israel, keep for your servant David my father the promises you made to him when you said, 'You shall never fail to have a man to sit before me on the throne of Israel, if only your sons are careful in all they do to walk before me as you have done.' And now O God of Israel, let your word that you promised your servant David my father come true.

—1 Kings 8:23–26

The first thing that Solomon does is remind God of a vision that was in his father's heart and the promise of God to fulfill that vision. David was not the one to see it come to pass but rather the one to lay the groundwork for his son to fulfill what he had labored for. David had prepared the blueprints as well as spent a good number of his years storing up the resources needed to fulfill the dream the Lord had given him. Solomon thanks the Lord for fulfilling His promise to David through him and declares that there is no God like the Lord, who keeps His covenants of love. He then goes on to ask the Lord to further keep His promises made to David. This is a clear example of two generations partnering to fulfill one vision.

Following the conclusion of Solomon's prayer in 1 Kings 9:4–5, God responds to Solomon. He declares to Solomon that he would be included in the promise given to David if he was faithful to walk in the decrees the Lord had given His father. Solomon was willing to honor the intended purposes of God in his father's life. It was the promise of God in his father's life that validated Solomon's destiny. What would have happened if Solomon were either unwilling or uninterested in his father's vision? What if Solomon never really listened to his father during those countless recitations of the Lord's promises to him? He could have thought to himself, "Sounds like a crazy dream, Dad, but I have good ideas of my own. I have been thinking of a lot of new things I could do as king." Rather, Solomon recognized the significance of what God was doing in the generation before him and was willing to play a part in its fulfillment. This allowed God to bless Solomon's life and the part that he would play in history.

Because God is a God of continuity, weaving one grand story throughout history, His church is best illustrated as one historical body passing the baton of God's covenants throughout the ages. Hebrews 11 recounts a tremendous history of faith spanning several thousand years. In Hebrews 11:39 through Hebrews 12:1, the scripture says:

> These were all commended for their faith, yet none of them received what had been promised. God had planned something better for us so that only together with us would they be made perfect. Therefore, since we are surrounded by such a great cloud of witnesses, let us throw off everything that hinders and the sin that so easily entangles, and let us run with perseverance the race marked out for us.

God has planned that each generation should play a part in finishing His story, displayed in previous generations. It not only reveals the continuity of God's actions but His covenant-keeping nature. The writer of Hebrews encourages us that because we have the ability to fulfill the promises given to men and women of faith who have gone before us, we must run that race marked out for us in history with perseverance. There is literally a cloud of witnesses spurring us on. In this long story of God's faithfulness on the earth, our lives represent one small verse. We are given center stage for one brief moment so that we might contribute our one musical note in the grand symphony of God's story. The individual notes of a musical masterpiece receive their beauty by the way they follow the notes that precede them and introduce the notes that follow. There is a race marked out for us, and its significance is in the way it fits into history. If we are to see our "land" blessed, then we must be willing to honor that history.

Several years ago, our Youth With A Mission center in Chicago began to feel a burden for the affluent businessmen and women of our city. We discovered that 94 percent of the millions who make up this sub-culture group in the cities of our country are unchurched. When we asked the Lord what we should do, we felt Him instruct us to target a downtown courthouse plaza with a method of evangelism used in our mission around the world called "Prayer Stations." There were many options of places that we could target, but the Lord consistently directed us to this location. Over the last ten years we have prayed with over 10,000 people in this plaza. Several times I wondered if we should go to a different location but always felt the Lord encouraging us to stay, and we have consistently sensed a willingness of the Lord to reveal Himself in this plaza.

It was not until last year that I stumbled across a story that shed some light on God's commitment to meet us at this location. In the book *Well with My Soul* by Rachel Phillips, the story is recounted of D. L. Moody, one of the great evangelists of the nineteenth century. He would preach to the wealthy businessmen of Chicago every day around noon on the courthouse steps at the corner of Randolph and Clark streets.[1] This is the same corner that we had sent our teams to for over ten years during the noontime hours, calling the business community back to God. As I read some of Moody's messages to the people of 1870, I could see the passion that the Lord had given him. Moody displayed a dream for the redemption of this people group in our city. God had covenanted with his obedience, and we were experiencing the fruitfulness of that covenant.

The next week when we went down to the plaza to do ministry, I stood on that corner and imagined Moody standing on his small platform preaching to those who walked by over 135 years ago, and

I began to weep. I prayed like Solomon, reminding God of His covenant with Moody and asking God to fulfill, in us, the burden that Moody carried for the redemption of this business community in our city. I sensed the Lord's pleasure. We give the Lord the opportunity to reveal His covenant-keeping nature when we honor the generations before us. If we are to see the redemption of God's purposes in our generation, we must be willing to connect with history.

You will recall the scripture in Psalm 68:6 that declares that God "sets the lonely in families." Again, the word translated "lonely" actually means "solitude" or "alone." The emphasis is not that God is primarily seeking to remove emotions of loneliness but rather that He seeks to connect us to family. It is not God's intention that anyone be alone. The importance of a family in biblical culture was not simply the relationships that were enjoyed. Rather, families have a history, a name, and an inheritance. A family's history represented its story of covenant with the Lord throughout generations. To be connected to that history gave each member of that family, throughout the generations, a connection to those covenants and the honor of fulfilling them. To have a family name meant that you had a destiny, that God had declared a unique calling on that family's role in His story of faithfulness on the earth. God connects us to families in order that we might have a sense of direction, an awareness of where God is leading us. There are no Lone Rangers in God's kingdom. Our personal destinies are intended to be connected to a bigger family of destiny. This allows for individual, unique gifting in a family to work together and bring about a synergistic beauty in that destiny. To have a family inheritance meant that there were promises that God had given the family. Those promises were transferred throughout generations as they continued in the faith. To not have an inheritance meant that you were deprived of the promises of God for your future fruitfulness in His kingdom. Therefore God sets us in families so that our "land," our personal vision and destiny, can be blessed and so that He may redeem the honor of those He has fashioned.

All of us have been connected, by the hand of God, to different families. We have authority to secure the honor of those families, ultimately securing God's honor as a covenant-keeping God and fulfilling His covenants on the earth. Our families can represent a physical family, spiritual family, ministry family, national family, or geographical family. Allow God to give you a sense of who you are by the families He has connected you to and the history that is represented through those families. God is looking for a generation that will be His agents of redemption through honoring the stories of faithfulness that have gone before. If we do not give weight, significance, and importance to the families that God has connected us to, then we are not honoring our fathers and mothers and are therefore separated from the blessings of God on our personal vision and destiny.

RESTORING BROKEN DREAMS

Often, the stories of faith throughout history have suffered loss or derailment. You may be connected to people, whether in your family, nation, or ministry, who were never able to see the fulfillment of God's calling and destiny on their lives. That fulfillment may have been robbed by injustice, tragedy, or even sin. We will experience God's redemption when we recognize His commitment to restore the broken down destinies of the past. Scripture indicates a calling on those whom God heals to repair and restore what has been lost.

Isaiah 61:4 declares of those whom the Lord has healed that "they will rebuild the ancient ruins and restore the places long devastated; they will renew the ruined cities that have been devastated for generations." Isaiah 58:12 speaks a promise to those who have walked in obedience to the Lord.

> Your people will rebuild the ancient ruins and will raise up the age-old foundations; you will be called the Repairer of Broken Walls, Restorer of Streets with Dwellings.

The Book of Nehemiah reveals the heart of one man who was burdened by the way God's purposes for Israel had been derailed. The children of Israel had been in captivity for seventy years. Finally, remnants under the leadership of Ezra were allowed to return to Jerusalem and rebuild the temple. But the walls were still broken down around Jerusalem, and those who lived there were subjected to threats and taunting by their enemies. They remained weak and vulnerable. Nehemiah cried out to the Lord to restore His destiny for Jerusalem and the children of Israel, to rebuild its walls, and fulfill and protect its purposes from the enemy. He identifies with the sin that had caused the derailment of that destiny but then appeals to God's nature to keep His promises to His people. In Nehemiah 9:7–8 we see the basis for Nehemiah's faith:

> You are the LORD God, who chose Abram and brought him out of Ur of the Chaldeans and named him Abraham. You found his heart faithful to you, and you made a covenant with him to give to his descendants the land of the Canaanites, Hittites, Amorites, Perizzites, Jebusites and Girgashites. You have kept your promise because you are righteous.

Nehemiah understood that God was faithful to honoring His promises. He was willing to play a part in God's desire to fulfill those promises in history. One of the greatest losses in tragedy is the inability to finish what was started. Before my wife died of cancer, she carried great dreams with God. She wanted to help her kids discover God and live lives of calling and intimacy with Him. She had a burden to see a generation of young people trained and sent as urban missionaries, working to redeem cities around the world. She had a deep burden for

Native Americans in our country with a longing to see their honor and destiny with God restored. She believed God had given her a calling to establish an outreach to those suffering with AIDS. What does God do with these dreams that were carried in faith? How are we to respond to the apparent derailment of those plans? After Sherry died, I rejoiced that she was with the one she loved the most. I could only imagine the joy she was experiencing in His presence. Yet somehow there was a sense of injustice. I felt that something had been stolen. Maybe it was her chance to live those dreams with God and have the honor of giving them to Him when she saw Him face to face. Maybe it was God's desire to watch her love Him, with obedience, in the burdens that He had given her.

God is a promise keeper. He defends our honor. If tragedy, loss, and evil can hinder God from fulfilling His promises or the intended honor of those who have gone before us, then He is not a redeeming God and is subject to our broken and fallen world. Rather, God creates the opportunity for that redemption to take place through us. At Sherry's funeral there was a room full of people who had experienced her heart for the things the Lord had given her. I recounted those burdens that she carried, and we all stood and asked the Lord to show Himself faithful to those purposes and her honor by fulfilling those visionary dreams. It was not only Sherry's honor that we were fighting for but also God's. He has the right to be seen as an all-powerful Redeemer. When we fight for the honor of those who go before us, then we are really fighting for the Lord's honor and right to be seen for who He truly is.

Recently, my daughter and I read a book together, *Almost Home*, written by Wendy Lawton. It recounts the story of Mary Chilton, who was a young girl on the *Mayflower*. The band of Pilgrims dreamed of a land where they could freely worship God and bring their children up in the faith. The Pilgrims had sacrificed much to make this journey to

America. Many died from sickness and disease along the way. Mary's own father and mother died during that journey. But they had told her many times the dream God had given them. Several months after Mary arrived, having barely survived the winter through the help of friendly Native Americans, the small community ordained a thanksgiving feast with over ninety of the natives joining them. As the preparations were being laid, Mary got an idea and went to her cabin to retrieve something belonging to her mother. It was a tablecloth her mother made. As she took it to the thanksgiving feast, knowing that this was her mother's dream, she whispered to her mother, who was no longer there, that she was beginning to understand. She realized that God was a master weaver, displaying His great pattern through the individual patterns that He weaves together. My daughter and I stopped reading and fought back the tears. It was a picture of God's commitment to honor the faith of those who have gone before us. In that act, Mary Chilton was honoring the life of her mother.[2]

How much of God's character do we display to the world when we honor the past? It is so much a part of God's heart that He promises blessing to us if we are willing to do it. It is the glory of every generation to rebuild the walls around the covenant promises of the generation before. As we look at the holes in the walls surrounding past dreams that have suffered loss, we can be tempted to build nests of resentment, unbelief, or fear rather than rebuild and protect God's covenant promises. This happens when we are unable to honor or give significant weight to the past. Not only does this grieve God, but it hinders Him from bringing forth fruitfulness in what He has invested. God is a God of history; therefore we consecrate old altars rather than bury or forget them.

It seems that our Western culture has defined maturity as that point at which we are able to leave our family and become independent, ready to make our own mark on the world. I would suggest that biblical maturity is defined by our willingness to move away from independence to an identity with a greater community. We are experiencing true maturity when we can recognize the significance of those who have gone before us and the part that we are to play in the broader continuing story of God on the earth. God places us in families for this reason. Genealogies are found throughout the Bible to show us how God's covenant nature was being fulfilled in history and to honor stories of faith.

DEFENDING HONOR

In Genesis 9 we read the account of Noah and his family as they exit the ark. The first thing that takes place is that God communicates His covenant with Noah. It is the same calling that He gave Adam and Eve in the Garden: "Be fruitful, increase in number and fill the earth" (v. 1). Noah was to continue in God's plan. Shortly after this we read that Noah plants a vineyard and gets drunk one night from the wine that he has made. Apparently he is extremely drunk because he is found lying naked by his son, Ham.

Have you ever wondered why Noah was drunk? We get no indication that this was a pattern in his life. He was found completely righteous by the Lord when asked to build the ark. It seems like he had everything going for him. He had seen the incredible provision of God for him and his family. He had been included in God's covenant plan for mankind. What led him to get so intoxicated that he was found lying on the ground completely naked? Perhaps he was overwhelmed by all the loss that he had witnessed. Perhaps he was struggling in his faith for the responsibility the Lord had given him. We really can't know, but we do know that something went wrong, and the emphasis of this passage is on how his three sons responded to his shame.

Ham saw Noah first and did nothing about it. He went to his brothers and said, "Hey, Dad really got wasted, and he's lying on the floor completely nude." Shem and Japheth quickly go and cover their father, walking backwards with the sheet so they will not see their father's shame. Consequently, Ham is cursed for his dishonor to his father. What was Ham's problem? The curse definitely seems harsh. It's his "land" that is cursed, his family that loses its blessing. Shem and Japheth, on the other hand, are blessed. Noah declares that their land should be increased. Not only was Ham unwilling to recognize the important destiny that the Lord had on Noah's life but was unwilling to protect or fight for that destiny. He dishonored his father.

It is not only those who have displayed great faith that we are called to honor, but those who may have been shipwrecked along the way. We have the ability to cover the shame of those who have gone before us and fight for their intended honor. If we think that to honor our father and mother means only to respect them and not talk back to them, then we run the risk of missing the very call to honor. Regardless of whether those around us are living out God's intended glory for their lives, we must recognize their significance and fight for its release. As David declared in Psalm 139, the days that God intended for us have been written before one came into being. This means that every person who ever lived had a destiny that God Himself dreamt for their life before they were born. For many, those destinies were stolen through loss, tragedy, sin, or injustice. May God redeem those destinies through us.

God is jealous over the honor of His creation. As we seek to find God's redemption in our broken world, we must be agents of God's honoring nature. We can play a part in releasing the honor of those who have gone before us. There are stories of great faith and stories of tragedy and derailment. It is a part of our calling to restore those desolate inheritances. Allow God to weave your calling and destiny into the great tapestry of His faithfulness on the earth. Every generation is tempted to sever themselves from the previous generations. We have bought into the lie that we are only free to pursue our destiny when we are on our own and separate from those who have gone before us. In actuality, our destiny is only secured to the degree that we are connected to history. May we be a generation that releases God to fulfill His covenants, made with past obedience, through us.

Lord, I thank You that You are a God who finishes what You have started. You are the same God yesterday, today, and forever. I want to see the redemption of those covenants and dreams that You gave to those who have gone before me. I allow You to use me to honor that story of faith. May the world see You for who You are. You are a Redeemer. You are the Promise Keeper. You are the One who honors. It is my desire to honor You.

CHAPTER 10

ENDURING OBEDIENCE

*Be patient, then, brothers, until the Lord's coming. See how
the farmer waits for the land to yield its valuable crop and
how patient he is for the autumn and spring rains. You too, be
patient and stand firm, because the Lord's coming is near.*

—JAMES 5:7–8—

*As you know, we consider blessed those who have persevered. You
have heard of Job's perseverance and have seen what the Lord
finally brought about. The Lord is full of compassion and mercy.*

—JAMES 5:11—

N OT LONG AFTER my wife died, I was asked by several people
if I thought I would continue in the missionary work that
she and I had been a part of for nearly twenty years. Others
encouraged me to take some time off so I could see things more clearly.
It seems that during times of great loss or tragedy we feel a need to
evaluate our lives and consider new direction. We may even feel that
God is using our tragedy to get our attention and reveal some new
plan for our lives. I would like to suggest that it is during those times
of great loss that we should stand our ground. The Bible reveals the
stories of many men and women of faith who persevered in the call
of God on their lives in the face of great hardship. Some wait entire

lifetimes to see the fruit of their labor and others spend their entire lives sowing into God's kingdom, leaving it to another generation to harvest the fruit. Consider Paul's encouragement in Galatians 6:9: "Let us not become weary in doing good, for at the proper time we will reap a harvest if we do not give up."

I'm amazed at the way Scripture displays God's patience throughout history. He often waited centuries for the fulfillment of what He put into motion through the affairs of men. Christ came four thousand years after God first gave His promise of redemption to Adam and Eve, and many of the promises given to the prophets remain still for another age. Yet everything God does is always at the proper time. According to Galatians 6:9, the fruit is lost only if we give up. God is an enduring God who displays long patience. In 1 Corinthians 13 we are given a thorough definition of love and, since 1 John 4:8 declares that "God is love," we can conclude that 1 Corinthians 13 is a description of God Himself. We are told in verse 7 that love "endures all things" (NKJV). The Greek word used here is the same as the one appearing in James 5:11 as "perseverance." It literally means "to remain where you are; abide; and have fortitude." In other words, God Himself will always remain where He is, fortified in His purposes, through all things. James 5:11 declares that those who persevere (remain steady, have fortitude, and abide) will be blessed because they will see what the Lord, who is full of compassion and mercy, will bring about. I have said earlier that I believe the enemy seeks to steal from us temporarily in hopes that he may rob something from God for eternity. The enemy succeeds only if we give up. We are encouraged in Scripture to persevere because God promises that we will always reap what we sow.

Throughout our time in ministry there were many occasions when Sherry and I would be asked how we were doing and our only response was, "We're still here." We may have been experiencing hardship or discouragement but perseverance became our weapon against the enemy. We simply were not going to give him the pleasure of robbing from God what He deserved. While living by faith in ministry, there were times when we ate peanut butter and jelly sandwiches for days. At other times, we didn't know if we would have enough money the next day for groceries. We experienced times of fruitfulness and times of discouragement. At times we were surrounded by faithful help, and other times we were all alone. Sometimes our family seemed in blissful harmony and at other times in total disarray. It was during many of those times that our only weapon was perseverance.

Our consistent and enduring obedience is a powerful tool in God's hands. Often it is only those who remain in the call of God on their lives through long obedience who have the benefit of seeing God's purposes fulfilled. The opening scripture in James 5:7–8 speaks of a farmer's patience in waiting for his harvest. Interestingly, the Greek word used here is a unique word meaning "long patience" or "to bear for a long time." The root word means "from a distance." In other words, the kind of patience needed to see the returns on our labor is a long patience, one that can wait for its return from a distance. Living in an age of ever increasing speed, we have become a generation that evaluates success based on the quickest return. Yet the kingdom of God often operates on a totally different timetable. It's not the quickest return that determines success, but a timely return—one that fits into God's timing. If we change our direction in ministry simply on the basis of how quickly we see results, then all the enemy needs to do is throw some hurdle in our path that will slow us down enough to feel the need to quit. Ultimately, God's plans for us will be stolen and God will experience the greatest loss.

But how do we cultivate perseverance in our lives? How do we stand our ground in the wake of great loss and tragedy? I have discovered that perseverance is not a personality trait. I am, by nature, a very compliant person. I have never had a stubborn personality. Rather, I was usually the one who would be happy to just peacefully comply with whatever was expected of me. Perhaps you can relate. Or, maybe you are one of those stubborn people who can hold onto something like a pit bull terrier. Regardless of your personality, I believe it has nothing to do with perseverance. Instead, our ability to stand firm and remain in the call of God on our lives through any circumstance is more accurately a response to our intimacy with the Lord. It is what God deposits of Himself in our hearts that produces perseverance.

IMMOBILIZING FEAR

As obvious as it sounds, it is still worth noting that you must take the first steps to commit to something before you can persevere. Without commitment, you cannot persevere, and, therefore, cannot see the promised reward of your labor. In this generation of broken promises and relationships, it may not be commitment that you are afraid of, but rather failure in commitment that immobilizes you. I believe this generation has both the passionate desire and the ability to commit to the things of God. They have, through experiencing the opposite, developed a jealous hunger to display lifelong commitment to something. At the same time, I have noticed an inability in many who have worked with us over the years to actually make that first step of committing to a specific call of God on their lives.

It seems that there is an underlying fear that we may do the very thing that repulses us and wind up divorcing that which we set out to do. Imagine the dismay at waking up shortly after your wedding and realizing that you accidentally married the wrong person! We can be immobilized by a fear of "accidentally" marrying the wrong vision and direction for our lives. After waking up to what we have done, we could never pull ourselves to divorce that calling, since it would be the greatest definition of failure to us. Therefore, though we are easily roused to action as a generation, ready to face the most extreme challenges and sacrifice, we simply cannot commit. We are bound by the fear that we may realize, at the end of our lives, we somehow missed our real calling.

Some of you may relate all too well with this fear. No matter how much the Lord has equipped us to radically extend His kingdom, if we are unable to take the first step, the enemy still wins.

In order to enter that race with perseverance we must allow God to remove our fear. God is committed to revealing His will for our lives. He is the Good Shepherd. If we are walking in a submitted relationship to His lordship and a desire to spend our lives on behalf of His purposes, then God holds it as His joyful responsibility to give direction. Proverbs 20:12 says, "Ears that hear and eyes that see—the Lord has made them both." In Isaiah 30:21 the Lord declares that a characteristic of His returned mercy and restoration for Israel would be that "whether you turn to the right or to the left, your ears will hear a voice behind you saying, 'This is the way; walk in it.'" God will give you direction. It is meant to be a point of intimacy with your God, not fear. As He shares His burdens with you, He will confirm it through His word and others. We do not have to worry that we will somehow accidentally choose the wrong direction for our lives.

What then remains is the challenge to display long patience in that calling. Don't allow the enemy the pleasure of robbing from God what belongs to Him. Perseverance is a powerful weapon in the kingdom of God and the tool that allows for His covenant-keeping nature and long story of faithfulness to be displayed throughout history. There have been great stories of perseverance recorded for us in recent years and some very good books on principles for longevity in our calling. I would like to suggest a few principles I believe are crucial for this generation as we seek to remain in the call of God in spite of loss, tragedy, or brokenness.

CIRCUMSTANTIAL DIRECTION

In 1 Kings 19, we read the story of Elijah following a great victory against the prophets of Baal. Elijah had challenged the false prophets of his day and seen fire rain down from heaven as a sign of the Lord's power. He was perhaps the most feared man in all of Israel. Yet Jezebel sees Elijah as the only thing standing in the way of her power and vows to hunt down and kill him. In verse 3, Elijah is overcome with fear and runs to the Lord in what looks like total depression. He simply says to the Lord that everything is against him and it would be better if he just died (v. 4). It's hard to tell what exactly causes Elijah to want to just give up. It would seem that it is not just his fear of Jezebel but perhaps the shame that he feels in the way he responded to her that is causing his depression. Nevertheless, Elijah's faith is shaken and he desperately needs to hear from the Lord.

The Lord's response is very different to what Elijah may have anticipated. God is not at all disappointed with Elijah but simply ministers to him, while ignoring his plea to end his life and remove him from his calling. After Elijah is fed by the Lord, he then travels forty days to Mount Horeb, "the mountain of God," and enters a cave to rest (v. 8–9). The fact that Elijah travels to Mount Horeb is an indication that he wanted God to speak to him. It was a place to meet with God and receive instruction. What follows provides a principle for receiving guidance from the Lord. Elijah has gone through a terrible time of depression and threats on his life. He needs to hear from God. Interestingly, God simply asks him, "What are you doing here, Elijah?" Have you ever been there? You may have experienced something traumatic or perhaps the accumulation of horrible circumstances. You run to God, choosing the most holy place possible, wanting some direction, and God simply asks you, "What are you doing here?" Your response may have been a lot like Elijah's. In effect, he simply responds, "Isn't it obvious, God? Why else would I be here? Can't you see I need some new direction?" Elijah says in verse 10:

> I have been very zealous for the LORD God Almighty. The Israelites have rejected your covenant, broken down your altars, and put your prophets to death with the sword. I am the only one left, and now they are trying to kill me too.

Notice how he starts by defending his long history of obedience and then by reminding the Lord how much of a problem the Israelites have become. Have you ever done that? I have. It's quite embarrassing when God doesn't exactly jump on your bandwagon! After Elijah defends his need for some new assignment, God tells him to go outside the cave and that He will appear to him. Next is a powerful lesson in hearing God's voice. Verses 11–13 state:

> Then a great and powerful wind tore the mountain apart and shattered the rocks before the LORD, but the LORD was not in the wind. After the wind there was an earthquake, but the LORD was not in the earthquake. After the earthquake came a fire, but the LORD was not in the fire. And after the fire came a gentle whisper. When Elijah heard it, he pulled his cloak over his face and went out and stood at the cave. Then a voice said to him, "What are you doing here, Elijah?"

First, God takes Elijah through this incredible object lesson and then asks the same question as before: "Why are you here?" It's as if the Lord is saying, "I know you have been through a great ordeal, Elijah, but I am not using those things to redirect you. There is no reason for you to be here!" Sometimes we feel that God is trying to get our attention through the tragic losses and challenges of life, when God's plans have not changed. Maybe it's because we think that God is in some way behind all our circumstances, or perhaps we just don't have the confidence that God could get our attention any other way. God was not in the earthquake. He was not in the earth-shattering wind. He was not in the fire. Instead, He was in the gentle whisper. Often, it's the enemy who shouts to get our attention, not the Lord. If we look for direction in our circumstances, then we run the risk of being carried away by any distraction the enemy or the world may throw at us.

When your world is broken and threatened, stand your ground. God has the ability to speak and cause you to hear. If He wants to redirect you, He will! I have heard people over the years say things like, "Well, I'm just going to go ahead with it. If the Lord wants to beat me over the head to tell me otherwise, He can," or, "I am really going through it; I guess God is trying to get my attention!" or, "That was very unexpected. I wonder if God is trying to say something to me!" The concern I have with this perspective is that if we are looking at our circumstances to get direction, you can be sure the enemy will accommodate you. We are placing a tool in the enemy's hands to derail us from God's call at a whim.

God is an intimate Father and Friend; He will speak to you as such. When I want my children to receive something of great importance from my heart, I look them in the eyes and speak to them intimately. If God has to use horrific and traumatic experiences to get our attention, then something is terribly wrong with our relationship, and terribly limiting about His governing ability. Psalm 32:8–9 states:

> I will instruct you and teach you in the way you should go;
> I will counsel you and watch over you. Do not be like the
> horse or the mule, which have no understanding but must be
> controlled by bit and bridle or they will not come to you.

It should be a rare exception to the rule that God uses the bit and bridle to get us to go where he wants us to go. Rather, it is God's design to instruct and counsel us in love. You can be assured that God will do that. He has promised to guide you. When your world is falling apart all around you and you run to the Lord for some new direction, do not be surprised if He asks, "What are you doing here?" More often than not, God simply wants us to "remain, continue to abide in, have long patience," and stand our ground.

EMBRACING GOD'S HEART

Often the greatest tool for perseverance during difficult times comes through the way God shares His heart with us. There had been more than one occasion when Sherry and I had our bags packed, so to speak, ready for God to give us some new direction. I remember one time, shortly after our second child was born, where we had literally placed our suitcase at the door. All that was left was to call our leaders and inform them, in the most spiritual way possible, of course, that we thought it would be best to give our ministry responsibilities to someone more suited for the job. We sat on the couch next to the phone in total discouragement. Nothing had gone as planned. We did not see the results we set out for, most of our team members had left us, and we had gone through a very trying financial time. I remember sitting there and distinctly hearing the Lord say to my heart, "Brad, what are you doing?" I began to justify in my mind why we had failed and were not the best choice for the job. Surely God agreed, I thought.

An interesting thing happened, though. God did not answer my reasoning. He just began to remind me of His heart for those to whom we had been called to minister. I heard Him speak to my heart about the thousands of Asian Indians living in our neighborhood, about the Lebanese who were moving into the neighboring community. I saw the faces of countless Jewish families down the street, walking to synagogues on Saturdays, and of the many Romanian families living in our multi-unit apartment building. My mind was flooded with the faces of those to whom we had come to minister, and all I could hear was God's heart for them. I began to weep. I longed to give God what He deserved. I had tried to justify our desire to quit and ended up begging God to let us stay. I looked at my wife knowing that there was no way we could trade the privilege God had given us to labor for His dreams.

It became a pattern that whenever we were discouraged or going through a very difficult time, wanting nothing more than to escape the demands of ministry, God would begin to remind us of all that He longed to do in our city. He would show us the faces of those we were ministering to and reveal His dreams for them.

God's call on our lives is first and foremost a call to intimacy. It's an invitation to embrace His heart and a longing to be reunited with those He lovingly created. We can often justify leaving responsibilities but may find it much harder to abandon God's dreams. I believe this was the key to Jesus' endurance. Hebrews 12:2 says, "Let us fix our eyes on Jesus, the author and perfecter of our faith, who for the joy set before him endured the cross." Consequently the word *endured* is the same Greek word that we defined earlier as "to remain, abide in, to have fortitude." Jesus found the strength to abide in His suffering because of the joy that was set before Him. It was not His duty that He focused on but the reward of redeeming those He had created. It was the faces of you and I and all the nations of the world that captured His gaze.

Perhaps our ability to persevere is directly related to our ability to see God's heart. John 15:15 reminds us that God's goal for our lives is friendship, not merely servanthood. A servant is consumed with the prospect of his own reward or punishment, while a friend is fixed on the happiness of the one he has befriended. Jesus said, "I no longer call you servants, because a servant does not know his master's business. Instead, I have called you friends, for everything that I have learned from my father I have made known to you." It is the knowledge of the Father's heart that produces a persevering spirit. If I am evaluating my own losses or rewards in ministry, then it is easy to make concessions when experiencing hardship. Often we can settle for less. We may not get the million-dollar prize, but we can still go home with half a million. When we are evaluating God's losses and rewards, it's hard to see Him worthy of anything less than the greatest of returns. Actually, God has created us with a passionate desire to die for His glory. When we focus on His heart, it triggers a response in us to want to give Him what He deserves. When God speaks of David in Acts 13:22 He says, "I have found David son of Jesse a man after my own heart; he will do everything I want him to do." It seems that David's ability to do anything the Lord asked of him was simply a response to being a man consumed with the Lord's heart.

Many have become familiar with the Moravian missionary movement of the 1800s. As young Moravian missionaries sold themselves into slavery, realizing it was the only way to share the gospel with slaves on the highly controlled islands of the Caribbean, their friends and families would ask them how they could give up their lives and endure such suffering. History records that their response was, "May the Lamb that was slain receive the due reward of His sufferings." I remember visiting a Moravian church while on an outreach to the island of Jamaica several years ago and thanking God for the enduring spirit of those young Moravian missionaries. Their eyes were on the dreams and passions of their God. I am convinced this is the only way to remain in the call of God and not be derailed by loss and tragedy.

After Sherry died, rather than feeling the need to redirect my family's calling, I found myself pleading with God to give us what we needed to continue. I had found no greater joy in life than embracing God's heart for His world. I wanting nothing more than to finish the race He had marked out for us. Because our ministry had never been simply a delegated responsibility or duty but rather an intimate response to a piece of God's heart that He had shared with us, it was never an option to leave it behind. It always seemed a ridiculous question to be asked how much longer we thought we would continue working in Chicago. The answer was simply, "Until we finish what God entrusted us to do."

As we focus on the joy that our long obedience brings to our heavenly Father, we will find the strength to persevere. It has nothing to do with our personality but with the intimate way that we carry God's heart for his world. I have a picture hanging on my wall of a European shepherd embracing a young lamb. The words written beneath are from the poet Zelda Fitzgerald. It says, "Nobody has ever measured, even poets, how much a heart can hold."[1] It reminds me of how our hearts were created with the capacity to carry things much bigger than ourselves. As great loss and tragedy seek to steal your privilege of finishing the race that God has marked out for you, remember the intimate things that the Lord shared with you, and embrace that privilege of giving Him what He deserves.

Experiencing God's Provision

I have suggested throughout this book that loss, tragedy, and hardship can steal much of what once gave us confidence and strength in our calling. Often, God's promised provision comes in unexpected ways. I have come to believe that one of our greatest provisions for perseverance and the ability to stand our ground in ministry comes from the people that God places in our lives. God has created us for community and therein resides one of our richest resources of grace. The characteristics of the first church in Acts 2 reveal some of what gave them the strength to withstand the intense persecution of their day. They enjoyed each other's fellowship and shared in each other's resources to meet the needs of the body.

One of my family's favorite TV shows is *Extreme Makeover: Home Edition*. Each week an unsuspecting family is awakened up by a busload of construction workers and designers ready to overhaul their home. The impacting part of each show is the story of the family being helped. They are chosen usually because of a great hardship or tragedy they are experiencing. The excitement of the show is not only the way the workers turn a desperate house into a place of incredible gadgetry and comfort in one week, but more specifically the way they minister to the unique needs of the family with a desire to remove some of their hardship and suffering. Usually, the team of workers and the family are in tears by the end of the show. Often, my kids and I are fighting back the tears as well. The reason this show is so moving is because it reveals the power and beauty of a community working to restore and rebuild the lives of those who suffer among us.

We are moved by stories of communities who work together to overcome incredible loss or tragedy; and we reward, with the greatest of honors, those who have helped to relieve suffering in some way. It is a part of our intended glory as those made in the image of God to bear one another's burdens. I have been asked several times over the last four years since Sherry died how my kids are doing. They truly are doing much better than I expected. Though they have had to walk through their grief in many different ways, it seems there has been an incredible grace on them. Looking back I feel that much of that grace has come through the close friends and coworkers in our ministry. One of the characteristics of Youth With A Mission, in which my family serves, has been the way it operates in community. We have several staff who live and fellowship closely with each other. This has provided a very large family for my kids. They have many brothers, sisters, aunts, and uncles, so to speak, who are always looking out for them and ministering to their needs in unique ways. They have stepped in on many occasions to help fill some of the voids left by the loss of Sherry in our lives.

This is the way God intended His people to operate. Our greatest enemy in loss is aloneness, first in the way it isolates us from God and secondly in the way it can isolate us from the community God has designed to be there for us. Without that community, we can miss the grace God has deposited for us in this broken world. One of our ministries at YWAM Chicago over the years has been to regularly visit the homeless living in parks or under bridges in our city. I have noticed that there is a small window of opportunity with most who find themselves homeless. It seems that if they do not find a way to make themselves vulnerable and reenter community within the first three months, then they often remain homeless for years. We are not only made for relationships, but it is usually through relationships that God intends to provide restoration and support during difficult times. Often the greatest barrier we face in seeing the homeless regain their sense of destiny and involvement in the world is a hard independence that begins to set in after several weeks on the streets. They find it easier to live alone than to make themselves vulnerable and let someone into their life of pain and struggle. Without knowing it, they put themselves on a path of slow suicide in regard to the unique image of God in their lives. They alienate themselves from the very thing that God has created for their strength: people.

We must recognize that one of our greatest strengths is community. We need to allow others into our broken world, and we need to practice radical generosity toward the needs of the family that God has put around us. By convincing us that we need to just buckle up and take care of things on our own, the enemy is able to steal what was intended to provide for enduring obedience in our lives. In Exodus 18:17–23, Moses is overwhelmed by the calling and responsibility the Lord had given him. His father-in-law recognizes Moses' weakness and says to him in verse 18, "You and these people who come to you will only wear yourselves out. The work is too heavy for you; you cannot handle it alone." He then instructs Moses to find men "who fear God" (v. 21) and share his responsibility with them. In verse 23 he says, "If you do this and God so commands, you will be able to stand the strain." God will use people to help us stand firm in our calling.

Although it is the Lord who jealously holds the honor of restoring to our soul all that we need to live a life of enduring obedience, He has placed us in families and community to provide strength and grace during loss. If we want to persevere in what God has entrusted to us, we must allow others into our lives and we must practice sensitivity and generosity to those God has placed around us. If we are so moved by the superficial attempts of the world to "bear one another's burdens" (Gal. 6:2, NKJV), imagine how powerful God's children could be if we revealed God's true greatness through brotherly love.

In order to find the redemption God has planned for our broken world, we will need to be a people of enduring obedience. Persevering in God's heart for the world is a part of our intended glory. We simply will not be able to see the grand returns of our labor without the commitment to bear for a long time the purposes of God. We will need to have the attitude of farmers, displaying long patience in the things God has entrusted to us. This is a generation equipped for commitment. As we walk in humility and abandonment, He will be faithful to speak His direction over our lives. We need to trust God and marry His dreams. Once we have embraced His calling on our lives, let us fix our eyes on the joy set before us, "that the Lamb who was slain may receive the due reward of His sufferings."[2]

Father, thank You for the intimate way that You guide me in my purpose and calling. May my hardship and loss never cause me to lose sight of Your heart and the privilege of following You. Don't let me be confused by the loudness of my circumstances but create in me ears to hear Your gentle whisper. Give me a heart of perseverance and long patience. Thank You for the family and community that You have placed around me. May I be a family and community to someone else who is suffering and experiencing the strain of loss.

CONCLUSION

*I prayed for this child, and the L*ORD* has
granted me what I asked of him.*

—1 S*AMUEL* 1:27—

*He raises the poor from the dust and lifts the needy
from the ash heap; he seats them with princes
and has them inherit a throne of honor.*

—1 S*AMUEL* 2:8—

T HE STORY OF Hannah in 1 Samuel 1–2 provides a powerful
reminder of God's commitment and willingness to redeem our
lives. Hannah had been married to Elkanah, an Ephramite,
for many years, but was barren and unable to give him a son. Like
the Shunammite woman we looked at earlier, Hannah's life was full
of shame in the culture of her day. She was unable to contribute to
the intended story of God's faithfulness through her family, although
Elkanah loved her dearly and pleaded with her to simply accept her
barrenness and be happy with his love. It was not enough.

God has created us for honor. Our honor lies in our ability to give
something of worth to the one who is the most valuable being in the
universe—something that would bring Him lasting happiness. It is this
intended honor that loss and tragedy threaten the most. Through the
mercy of God, He has put a limit on how long we live in this suffering
world. And, He has given us the opportunity through the work of the
cross to trade our short, fleeting existence on this earth for a long

existence with Him in eternity some day. Yet our short life on this earth provides the only opportunity we have to display the worth and value that we place on our God. Too often we make concessions in our difficult circumstances. We can have a hard time seeing the Lord accurately in our loss and lose our confidence to finish the race that was once marked out for us.

There is a heart cry in this generation to find some way to rise above its devastating losses and seize something of meaning and purpose for their lives. I have been intrigued by the kind of heroes that have grabbed the attention of this generation over the last several years. Often what makes its way into the mainstream of entertainment and art can be a good reflection of what a culture struggles and identifies with. The heroes we create are those we most want to be like and those who give us some hope of what we can become. They almost always represent those who are not only the most unlikely of heroes but also those who have either suffered insurmountable hurdles or simply do not have what is normally needed to become something greater than who they feel they are. We can identify with the overwhelming personal losses that our heroes have experienced. We often live through them the dream of somehow overcoming those losses and making a lasting impact in the world. It strikes a chord in the tension we feel between how small and vulnerable we are and the glory and destiny our hearts tell us we were made for. Yet many struggle with a real fear of never recovering from the hurts and pains of the past.

We are haunted by the thought of looking back on our lives someday only to discover that we have accomplished nothing of lasting value. The character Éowyn, in Peter Jackson's movie version of *The Lord of the Rings* by J. R. R. Tolkien, eloquently spoke what I believe many feel. She longed to fight in the epic battle against the dark lord of the land, ready to give her life for truth and justice. When asked by the returning king, Aragorn, what she feared the most, her reply was, "A cage; to stay behind bars until use and old age accept them, and all chance of valor has gone beyond recall or desire."[1] Our losses can become cages over time that keep us locked up and separated from our destiny with God. God has paid a price for the redemption of our broken and shattered lives. He longs to return to us a hope and expectation for those things from which we have been alienated.

The spirit of Hannah challenges me. She would not settle for second best. She knew her destiny enough to seek God for her honor. The Scripture tells us that she continuously cried out to the Lord to remove her shame. She declares in 1 Samuel 1:16, "I have been praying here out of my great anguish and grief." She simply wants the chance to give something that will honor her God. As I walked through the loss of Sherry, there was a mounting cry in my heart that could not have been put into words. I felt my fruitfulness challenged like never before, I felt my kids' destinies threatened, and I longed for Sherry's intended honor not to be lost. For the first several months, I could not even communicate the depths of my longing to see all that God had intended for my family secured once again. One evening, months later, I stood in my living room, longing to cry out to my God and my Redeemer. I opened my mouth and all that came was a deep wailing cry. I was unwilling to concede the destiny of my family in our loss. I desperately cried to God to redeem. When I was done I felt a release, not so much on my heart, but from the Lord's heart. It was as if He had been waiting for me to approach Him with the kind of desperation that matched His jealous desire to redeem and restore. In fact, it was God who was unwilling to concede!

Do you feel threatened by the losses you have experienced? Are you overwhelmed by all the loss you see in the world around you, unable to put into words the burden you feel? God is a redeemer. He has bought back our destiny with Him. Regardless of loss, tragedy, or failure, He has the ability to secure your fruitfulness. He is not out of control because nothing can separate us from His loving commitment to our restoration and honor. He waits only to be invited in. Unless we focus our circumstances on His redeeming nature, we can lose our expectation of Him to respond to all that has been robbed from us.

God answered Hannah's cry and birthed Samuel through her. God not only gave her a son, but one of the most anointed and influential leaders in Israel's history. Where are the Samuels of our day? Have you asked God for your Samuel? I am suggesting that our expectation of God often does not match the greatness of His commitment toward us. John 15:16 says that God has appointed us to bear fruit. To say that loss or tragedy can steal that destiny lessens God's greatness. The glory of God is wrapped up in the way He responds with power in our broken lives. God identifies with our sorrow because He shares in the loss of what His original intent was for our world. He weeps with us. Yet His sorrow always moves Him to action. How great is your expectation on God to redeem your intended honor and fruitfulness before Him?

I find it interesting that God does not rebuke Hannah for her desperate plea. When Eli the prophet finally realizes what Hannah is crying out for, he does not give her a lesson on just accepting her lot with thankfulness and contentment. Rather, he simply says, "Go in peace, and may the God of Israel grant you what you have asked of him" (1 Sam. 1:17). Eli affirms the rightness of Hannah's cry, and God does answer. He not only redeems Hannah's fruitfulness but also releases His plans for the children of Israel through the answer to her prayer. Hannah was bold enough to bother God. In 1 Samuel 2:8 we see the basis of her faith. She declares of the Lord, "He raises the poor from the dust and lifts the needy from the ash heap; he seats them with princes and has them inherit a throne of honor." Her faith in God's redeeming nature gave her the expectation that He would hear her cry and therefore the perseverance to continue pursuing Him for her destiny.

Is there anguish in your soul over what you have experienced? Allow the revelation of who God is to cause you to seek Him for the redemption of your fruitfulness and your intended honor of finishing the call of God on your life. God does not want you to ignore, belittle, or get over your loss. He desires to share that loss with you and to intimately colabor with you to do something about it. He will restore your soul, giving back to your inner being everything you need to finish writing His story on your life. It is a part of our intended glory to reveal God's story of faithfulness on the earth. I am suggesting that we do that by becoming agents of redemption both in our own lives as well as in the world. Because God is a redeemer by nature, our tragic losses actually give us the authority to call upon His name and invite the manifestation of that powerful nature in the circumstances of our broken world.

We will discover that redemption as we: fight for our own fruitfulness; seek to defend His greatness by exposing the futility of the enemy's claims; allow God the only honor of filling the voids in our lives left through loss and tragedy; connect to the Lord's covenants with past obedience, being willing to be the return on investments the Lord has made throughout history; honor the story of God's faithfulness in the generations that have gone before us by restoring desolate inheritances and fighting for God's original dreams; and respond to God's call on our lives with long obedience through embracing God's heart. The emphasis of Scripture is on a God who responds to our losses and partners with us to bring about redemption in our world. May we be a generation who can move beyond our losses and be as jealous over the Lord's desire to bring about that redemption as He is.

At times, I still feel like that little boy who has just had the breath knocked out of him by the school bully. But now, I am no longer powerless to respond, because of this assurance to me from God:

> For I am convinced that neither death nor life, neither angels nor demons, neither the present nor the future, nor any powers, neither height nor depth, nor anything else in all creation, will be able to separate us from the love of God that is in Christ Jesus our Lord.
>
> —Romans 8:38–39

NOTES

INTRODUCTION

1. Harold Ivan Smith, *Grievers Ask* (Minneapolis: Augsburg Fortress, 2004), 108–109

Chapter 2
A PARTNER IN SORROW

1. Smith, *Grievers Ask*, 40–41

2. C. S. Lewis, *The Voyage of the Dawn Treader* (New York, NY: HarperCollins, 1994), 88–91.

Chapter 4
UNDERSTANDING REDEMPTION

1. Noah Webster, *American Dictionary of the English Language* (New York, NY: Converse, 1828), s.v. "redeem."

Chapter 9
REDEEMING HONOR

1. Rachel Phillips, *Well with My Soul* (Uhrichsville, OH: 2004), 14–15.

2. Wendy Lawton, *Almost Home* (Chicago: Moody Publishers, 2003), 134.

Chapter 10
Enduring Obedience

1. Zelda Fitzgerald, famous quote, http://www.quotes andsayings.com/gpromise.htm, (accessed March 14, 2008).

2. Taken from the message "Ten Shekels and a Shirt" by Paris Reidhead, found at http://www.dccsa.com/greatjoy/ 10Shekels.htm.

Conclusion

1. *The Two Towers*, dir. Peter Jackson (New York, NY: New Line Cinema, 2001), based on the book by J. R. R. Tolkien.

TO CONTACT THE AUTHOR

To learn more about Brad Stanley's ministry:

www.ywamchicago.org

To find more on God's redeeming commitment to us:

www.unwillingtoconcede.com

If you would like to contact Brad Stanley or share your story:

ywamchicago@aol.com